The Choy of Seafood

Other Books by Sam Choy:

Sam Choy's Cuisine Hawaii
With Sam Choy, Cooking from the Heart
The Choy of Cooking, Sam Choy's Island Cuisine

Recipes and Text Copyright © 1998
by Sam Choy

Above: Hand-carved model of Hawaiian
outrigger canoe by artist Francis Pimmel,
Wahiawa, Oʻahu.

Additional photo credits:
Raymond Wong: portrait, xii; background
    photos; 2, 28, 52,72, 96, 118, 146, 168
Michael Stewart: 116-117
Gary Hoffheimer: 144-145
Wine bottle photos appear courtesy of
    E. & J. Gallo Winery.

Library of Congress Catalog Card
Number: 98-67135

Casebound
ISBN 1-56647-173-7

Softcover
ISBN 1-56647-222-9

First Printing, October 1998
Second Printing, December 1998
2 3 4 5 6 7 8 9

Mutual Publishing
1215 Center Street, Suite 210
Honolulu, Hawaii 96816
Telephone (808) 732-1709
Fax (808) 734-4094
e-mail: mutual@lava.net

Printed in Hong Kong

THE CHOY OF SEAFOOD

BY SAM CHOY

MUTUAL PUBLISHING

THE CHOY OF SEAFOOD
OF SEAFOOD
SAM CHOY'S PACIFIC HARVEST

BY SAM CHOY

Written by
U'i and Steven Goldsberry

Production Coordination by
U'i Goldsberry

Photography by
Douglas Peebles

Book Design by
Gonzalez Design Company

Food Styling by
Faith Ogawa

GALLO *of* SONOMA

Mahalo

It's with sincere gratitude and appreciation that we say **Mahalo** to each and every one of you who contributed your time, talents, energy, and Hawaiian treasures to the success of *The Choy of Seafood*. Mahalo nui loa from the bottom of our hearts!

Ailene Steele
Aiyaz Dean
Alex Ka'au, Makana O Hawai'i,
    Mauna Lani Bay Hotel and Bungalows
Alice Yamaguchi
Amy Ogawa
Amy Rosato, Island Orchid
Amy Tanaka
Anne Inouye
Ashley Kirk
Ashley Wong
Audrey Wilson, Coca-Cola Bottling
    Company of Hawai'i
Barbara Underwood
Betsi Kohler, Betsi's Bowls
Bev Onaha
Bill Kirk
Billy Mitchell
Bob Powers
Bob Yurth, Waiu Kahe Farm
Bonnie Miki, Kona Kapa, Inc.
Brenda Schott, Under the Koa Tree
Bryant Spurrier
Candice Lee
Capt. Mike Remer, Mariner's Canteen
Carlos Hernandez, Liberty House
Carol Choy
Carol Yurth, Waiu Kahe Farm
Carrie Lee Lickle, Hawaiian Fish Prints
Carter Miller
Catherine K. Spurrier
Cecil DelCarmen
Charles Cosgrove, Liberty House-
    Kailua-Kona
Chef Paul Muranaka
Chef Troy Terorotua
Chef Willie Pirngruber,
    Hilton Waikaloa Village
Christopher Choy
Clairemoana Choy

Cora Buno, North Hawai'i
    Community Hospital
Courtney Paaga
Craig Sako
Cynthia and Kent Inouye
Dan De Luz, Dan De Luz's Woods, Inc.
Dane Otani, Coca-Cola Bottling
    Company of Hawai'i
Daniel "Kaniela" Akaka, Jr., The Mauna Lani
    Bay Hotel and Bungalows
Darlene Nakasone
David R. Shiigi, Bromeliads Hawai'i
David Souza
Dean Edgerton, Jr.
Dean Ka'ahanui, Ka'ahanui Kreations
Debbie Wong
Deedee Ogawa
Deedee Yamaguchi
Denise Paaga
Denise Truck
Dick and Shelly Hershberger,
    Creative Greenery
Dr. Cheryl Gaebel
Don Dickhens, General Manager,
    Mauna Lani Hotel and Bungalows
Don Yun
Doris Murakami and Ohaha
Dustin Y. Ebesu
Dylan Spurrier
Eddie Fernandez
Edible Delights
Eileen Tredway
Elizabeth Lee, Malu's Enterprise
Eric S. Tanouye, Green Point Nursery
Ernest Miller
Fia Mattice, Volcano Art Center
Flying Seafood, Inc.
Frances Woodland
Francis Pimmel
Gallery of Great Things
Garrett Wong
Garth Spurrier
Gary Wagner, Plaza Pacific Design
Gene St. Hilaire, Costco-Kona
Georgia Sartoris, Georgia Sartoris Fine Art
Gerald A. Ben, Ben Woodworking
Gerardo Hermosillo

Glen Arakaki
Harriet Goldsberry
Harry Ogawa
Harvey M. Sacarob, Sun Bear Produce
Haunani Goldsberry
Haunani Manning
Hawaii State Archives, for historical photos
Herbert Naeole, Foodland Supermarket, La'ie
Hilton Waikaloa Village, Management
    and Staff
Hina Lei Creations
Hoku Choy
Holly Wheeles
Howard Deese, State Department of
    Business, Economic Development,
    and Tourism
Howard Spurrier
Ichiro Yamaguchi
Ikuko Bacon
Jack Gillen
James Lee
James McCully, Orchid Culture
Jamie Wong
Jan Charbonneau
Jane Fishback
Janice Akioka
Jean Nakahara, Antiques Sakae
Jeanne Carroll, Vision Beads
Jeff Chang, Jeff Chang Pottery
Jeffrey Keiji Lee
Jeffrey B. Martin, Aloha Airlines
Jennifer Pontz, Tropical Art Glass
Jenny Mitchell
Jim Verhoeven
J.K. Spielman
John S. Piert, Piert Woodworking
John Tanaka
Jolyn Goldsberry
Jonell Guzman
Joni Spurrier
Joseph R. Spurrier
Julie Tubb
Junko Weeks, Jun Silks
Kahlil Dean
Kahuku Harvest Inc.
Kaimele McClellan,
    King Kamehameha Hotel

Kalani DeWitt, Hawaiian Fish Prints
Kamiko Akioka
Kamran Mohager, Home-Tech Inc.
Karl Drew
Karon Chang, Jeff Chang Pottery
Katie Spurrier
Kelvin T. Sewake, University of
    Hawai'i-Manoa
Ken Hufford
Kenny Tilton
Kersten Johnson
Kevin Nutt, West Hawaii Foodworks
Kim Goldsberry
Kimberly Yancey
Kimo Spencer, Under the Koa Tree
Kona Crew at Sam Choy's Cuisine Restaurant
Kona Mushrooms, Inc.
Kramer Paaga
Kristen Kofsky, Kofsky Fine Arts
Kristene Short
Kyle Ino, Kyle Ino Designs
Kyle Spurrier
Laura Tappe
Leanne Kirk
Lehua Sen
Lavina Wong, Liberty House
Liko Harwood
Linda Bong
Linda Miller
Lindsay Goldsberry
Lisa Adams, Spiral Triangle Studios
Liz Hersage
Loretta Viecelli, "Viecelli"
Lyle Moody
Lyman Medeiros
Lynne Herron, The Showcase Gallery
Maha Kraan
Maile Spurrier
Mamo Howell, Inc.
Manuel Guzman
Marie Brick, Gallerie of Great Things
Marie McDonald
Mark McGuffie, Mauna Lani Bay
    Hotel and Bungalows
Mary Ann Pyun
Mary Lou De Luz, Dan De Luz's Woods, Inc.
Mary Lou Lain

Mary Remer, Mariner's Canteen
Matsuko Shigemasa and Ohaha
Mauna Lani Bay Hotel and Bungalows,
    Management and Staff
Megan Manning
Mel Arelano
Micah Goldsberry
Michael Horton
Michael Manning
Michael Prine, Strawberry Hawai'i, Inc.
Michael Wong
Mike Rosato, Island Orchid
Mindy Raymond
Mr. and Mrs. Yuki Togo
Momi Green, Greene Acres
Nahinu James
Nakano Farms
Nancy James, Host Marriott
Napua James
Natasha Miller
Nathan James
Neal Matsumura, Big Island Laminates
Nicolette Hermosillo
Nina Millar
No'eau James
Nohea James
Norman "Buzzy" Histo,
    Kalikokalehua Hula Studio
Nora Kirk
Paniau
Patrick Choy
Peggy Chesnut, Chesnut and Company
Peggy Wallace, Upcountry Connection
    Gallery
Pi'i Laeha
Randy Echito
Raymond M. Yamasaki, Ray's Oriental
    Designs
Renee Dyer
Renee Fukumoto-Ben
Rick and Roxanna Moss
Rick Clark, "Hawaiiana" Vintage Items
    Collection
R. Jeff Lee, Lee Ceramics
Roen Hufford
Roger Jellinek
Roger Pogline, Moon Road

Ron Okumura
Ronald Y. Hanatani, RYH Pottery
Ross Moody
Roxanne Yun
Sam Choy, M.H.K.
Samuel Spurrier
Scott Goldsberry
Scott Nakasone
Setsuko Wong
Sharon "Setekh" Outcault
Shawn Okumura
Shirley Okumura
Stephen Kofsky
Steven Akioka
Steven A. Katase, Royal Hawaiian
    Sea Farms
Steven Inouye
Susan James
Taylor Goldsberry
Teresa Verhoeven
Terry Taube
Thomas Shoda
Thomas K. Spurrier
Thomas Wong
Tim Nelson
Tom Baynes, Liberty House—
    Kailua-Kona
Tom Pico
Tomlietta Rosehill
Toni Ann Souza
Toni Mallow
Tony Harwood
Trent Wong
Trevor Nakasone
Trinity Wong
Troy Okumura
Tyson Nakasone
Upcountry Connection Gallery
Van P. Atkins
Volcano Art Center
Wai Lin Choy
Wai Sun Choy
Wayne Hyna
Wes Sen
Wesley Sen
Wilbur Won, Hawai'i Art Gallery
Yuki Shigemasa and Ohana

Dedication

I dedicated both of my previous Mutual Publishing cookbooks to my family, Mom and my late Dad (especially Dad in the second book); to my wife Carol; my sons Sam, Jr. and Christopher; my sisters Wai Sun and Wai Lin; and my brother Patrick. I also mentioned our capable local farmers and fishermen, and the hard-working people of Hawai'i.

I remember all these important, deeply loved folks again, because no way would I be able to write these cookbooks without them.

But this one I dedicate to Hawai'i's fishermen—not all of our fishermen, but most—the ones who understand and practice a wise husbandry in our precious fishing grounds.

Over the last few years, with the appearance of long-line multi-hook trolling and drift-net "curtain of death" fishing techniques in our coastal waters and the Pacific at large, certain fish populations have declined dangerously.

Even sustenance fishermen, a few of them, have over-fished the reefs. Or worse: some have used poisons that indiscriminately kill everything they touch, including coral polyps.

The State of Hawai'i and the Federal government have taken strong action enforcing our marine conservation laws. I fully support all their efforts. And I support expanding enforcement and education programs not only here in Hawai'i Nei, but among our sister countries along the Pacific Rim. We should fund marine research and restocking programs; make better use of fish by-products in our markets; ban the sale of shells and coral trees throughout the Islands.

What I've learned from a lifetime of fishing is that everything in the ocean is connected and interdependent. The health of a school of aku (bonito tuna) off French Frigate Shoals affects the runs of marlin near Kailua-Kona. A dying reef on Windward O'ahu harms flying fish in the Hawaiian Deep.

Balance is the key. Ancient Hawaiians certainly understood this and would place a kapu (taboo) on a fish species during spawning season. Theirs was a craftsman-like harvest of the waters. Let their successes guide us in managing our fisheries.

So, to those men and women of the sea who appreciate the invaluable and essential gifts of our fish families—to those who have learned to give back what they take—I dedicate *The Choy of Seafood* and all of my future endeavors as a seafood chef.

Contents

Introduction

In the Islands we say, "Lucky you live Hawai'i." I am so fortunate to have grown up here. Our waters and reefs produce some of the most spectacular seafood in the world. We get up in the morning, drive to the harbor, and watch the boats come in, all loaded down with the catch. In about an hour, the fish are weighed and lined up on the dock: tubs of aku and 'o'io, rows of iced 'opakapaka and steel-blue ono, and hanging on the suspended scale, a 200-pound 'ahi. My restaurants alone buy over 3,000 pounds of fish a week.

Really, the ocean is our backyard, and our front yard.

I was raised on the island of O'ahu, in a small town called La'ie. If you drive north on Kamehameha Highway from Kane'ohe toward Sunset Beach, you can't miss it. I spent most of my growing up years on Hukilau Bay. On the map it's called "La'ie Bay," but everyone who lives there calls it "Hukilau."

When I was little, every Saturday was Hukilau Day. A hukilau is a traditional community fish harvest, where sometimes a hundred people pull a huge net in from the waters offshore. Busloads of tourists came to the beach to watch our weekly hukilau and, if they wanted, they helped haul in the catch. The nets were always filled with fish: manini, uhu, awa, enenue, all kinds. We sorted the catch and distributed it to the neighbor people who helped. That bay provided a lot of food for the village.

There was Polynesian entertainment, and all the little kids and their families danced and played music. It was really a community affair. My parents were in charge of the food concession.

I went to the beach every chance. I loved walking the reef with a glass-bottomed box to go "squidding." The folks in Hawai'i call octopus "squid." It's a localism. Of course we know the difference, but everyone still calls it squid. So, we'd walk along the reef at low tide with a squid box in one hand, spear in the other. Sometimes, if you didn't have a box, you could chew coconut and spit it on the water and the oil in the coconut would make the surface clear so you could see, like magic, to the bottom. You have to go early, before the reef really gets going. (You know, there's nothing like smelling salt air coming in off the water in the morning.) If you have a good "squid eye," you can spot the octopus trying to camouflage itself in the reef, changing its colors as it moves.

Just outside of Hukilau Bay and off to the right, it gets really deep. A little sea mount pops straight up, out of nowhere, all crusted over with coral. There's great fishing out there: all kinds of reef fish, and underneath there are little shelves and pukas packed with lobster. It's just antennas, legs, and claws everywhere, kind of scary.

When we went lobster fishing we wore work gloves to protect our hands from the spiny shells, and we'd just pluck up enough bugs—we called them bugs—for dinner. But that was Hukilau in those days. Good fish, plenty of lobster. And all kinds of limu, the seaweeds, growing on different parts of the reef; and wana, the sea urchins with the sharpest spines, bristling in their little holes. We fished and swam and fished. It was like heaven: blue water, blue sky, white clouds, and white sand.

When I got older, I learned to surf. I surfed every day from age eleven until I got serious about cooking. I think I was about twenty-two.

There are three main surf breaks at Hukilau. When you face the ocean, on your far left is Goat Island. That's where I cut my head on the reef and got coral stuck in my back and almost died. I got crunched by a hollow four-foot wave at super-low tide and I slammed into the reef. When I paddled back out, one of my friends said, "Hey, Sam, you're all bleeding! That's going to attract sharks!" But I stayed out because the surf was so clean and good, and no sharks came.

In the center of the bay is Middle Break. It's in deep water and kind of a far paddle. To the right is Janet Gaynor's break, named after the famous movie star. She had a vacation house on the beach there, and straight out was that good surf spot. My friends and I even started The Janet Gaynor Surf Club. Today the kids call the break, pidgin-style, Jennagayta.

I surfed the North Shore a lot too, like at V-land, Sunset, Pipeline, Chun's Reef, 'Ehukai. My all-time favorite spot was Hale'iwa: great waves and great memories. Even though I don't surf at all now, I want to get back to it someday. You know, lose a little weight, jump back on the board.

I sit on Hukilau beach today and watch the water. The place hasn't changed too much, except some of the limu beds are gone. But I know what spots in the reef I can find weke, and where the manini hang out. In the bluest part of the bay is the lobster mount.

The whole time I was growing up I lived in the water, and I guess that's where I picked up my love for fish. Since I became a chef, it's been seafood that I like cooking the best. I love the way a good fresh fish looks, the feel of it, the weight, texture, the clarity of the flesh, the flavors, and how the meat accepts any seasonings. I love watching deep red 'ahi fillet fry. The dark pink-red meat slowly turns gray, almost like smoke rising into a red sunset sky. Then the juices sizzle and the fish gets crisp on the outside. There's an aesthetic quality to cooking it.

Hawai'i is unique in the way we've blended our ethnic foods. Each group has contributed a seasoning, a style of cooking, or a mixture of flavors to make local cooking as colorful as Hawai'i's people. I've combined these elements and developed my own "Kona Cuisine." Recipes like "Ginger Pesto-Crusted 'Opakapaka with Coconut Cream Sauce," and "Sam's 'Local Boy' Cioppino"—take traditional ingredients to make a new-but-old dish.

This book is my chance to showcase the artistry of these Islands, and introduce our local fish: 'ahi, aku, real 'opakapaka (not the red snapper or near snapper), weke 'ula, kalekale, 'o'io, and 'ula'ula. If your head's swirling with these strange-sounding names, don't worry. The recipe pages tell you their other names and what the fish look and taste like. A lot of Mainland fish can be used as substitutions for the ocean fish in the recipes. Pike, salmon, halibut, or blue fish can take the place of 'opakapaka. All the ingredients you need you should be able to find in any supermarket.

Seafood isn't just my specialty, it's my love. Ever since I started putting out my cookbooks, I've wanted to do one about just seafood. And this is it, finally!

I welcome you to try these recipes and taste how this nutritionally valuable meat can be made more incredible than you ever imagined. With my Kona Cuisine recipes, you're going to learn the true meaning of the word 'ono (delicious).

ONE

APPETIZERS

Shoreline Fishing

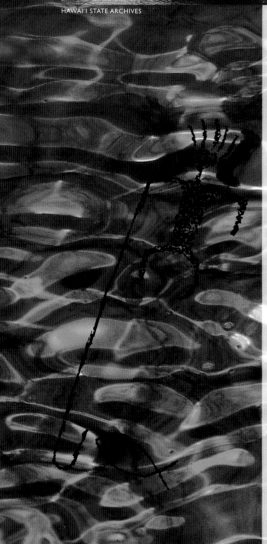

Fishing from the shore with a long pole has its own drama and kind of magic. In many ways it's fishing at its most fundamental, because the fisherman is confined to his place, the land, and he must cast out into the fishes' domain and see what he can catch.

Certain parts of the island offer certain kinds of fish. Off leeward points there are papio, off windward bays you find mullet, at cliffs where the water drops deep there'll be ulua. From piers you can get sand fish, 'o'io, and weke 'ula. You should talk to the locals to find out where a particular fish likes to hang out, but sometimes you know through experience what to expect in sheltered bays or open bays, coral bottoms or sand, water near muliwai (estuaries), deep water windward or leeward, off rocks or sandy beach.

There's a place near South Point, Hawai'i, that is famous for ulua. These are the crevalle or jack, and they can grow to five feet and over 100 pounds, and they're fighters. I once had a hit at South Point and the ulua was so strong I realized "there's no way I can bring him in, he just keeps taking line," so I cut him free.

But I've also pulled in my share of big ones, and smaller ones, like papio, which are young ulua.

Different fish require different poles and line, bait and sinkers. For menpachi and 'opelu, the mackerel scad, you go out at night. Pitch dark nights, put up a lantern on shore and the fish see it and come near.

I was out one night when the water filled with huge fins; I got scared, I thought it was sharks. But they were manta rays, their wings rising, and I saw the white underneath and knew they were mantas and not shark fins. Anyway, we were fishing for menpachi that night. When you throw your line, you should have a golf ball on it so it doesn't sink fast, and a glow bead to attract the menpachi.

Pole fishing can be pretty relaxing. No boat to worry about, no net to drag in and untangle. Some folks think the fishes you catch from shore aren't as good as deep-water kind. But if you cook them right, they're just as succulent and tasty.

Breakfast, Lunch and Crab's Crab Cakes
with Curry Aioli

Serves 6

I have had so many requests for this recipe since our restaurant in Iwilei opened. I demonstrated it on my KHNL television show, but still there are requests. I decided that putting it in my seafood cookbook was the best way for everyone to get it. So, here it is. Enjoy!

1 pound crab meat
1 dash of Worcestershire sauce
1 dash of Tabasco
1 tablespoon ogo
1 teaspoon curry powder
1 teaspoon dry mustard
1 tablespoon scallion, chopped
1 tablespoon red bell pepper, diced
1 teaspoon panko (Japanese-style crispy bread crumbs)

1/4 cup mayonnaise
1 teaspoon Magic Spice Mix (see recipe below)
1 cup all-purpose flour
1 cup Clarified Butter (see recipe below)
salt and pepper to taste
Curry Aioli (see recipe below)

> Crab meat is sold year round in Hawai'i. You can get it in the meat and fish sections of your favorite grocery store, in the frozen foods section, or in cans near the canned tuna. The canned meat is cooked, heat pasteurized, and vacuum-sealed to ensure its freshness. So be careful. Once it's opened, it should be used within 2 to 3 days.

Remove all shells from crab. Fold Worcestershire sauce, Tabasco, crab meat, ogo, curry powder, mustard, scallions, bell pepper, panko, mayonnaise, and Magic Spice Mix together. Form into patties, 4 ounces each. Dredge in flour and sauté in Clarified Butter. Arrange crab cakes on platter, and drizzle with Curry Aioli.

Magic Spice Mix:

1 teaspoon garlic powder
1 teaspoon onion powder
1 teaspoon Old Bay Seasoning
1 teaspoon paprika
1 teaspoon cayenne powder

Blend.

Clarified Butter:

1 cup butter

Melt butter in microwave oven. Heat for 1-1/2 minutes. Remove, and let set for 20 minutes. Carefully skim to remove the whey.

Curry Aioli:

1 cup mayonnaise
1/4 cup fresh cilantro, chopped
1 teaspoon rice vinegar
1 teaspoon fresh lime juice
1 teaspoon curry powder
1 teaspoon sesame oil
salt and pepper to taste

Blend, and set aside for about 30 minutes.

Antique fish trap–provided by Danny Akaka, Hawaiian Historian at the Mauna Lani Bay Hotel and Bungalows, Kohala Coast, Big Island.

Steamed Ama Ebi
with Dipping Sauce

4

Ama ebi is the Japanese name for the large, red-skinned shrimp we use here in the Islands. Hawai'i's main supply is harvested off the coast of Kaua'i. Commercial fisheries have started to produce brackish-water ebi, but I like the naturally sweet flavor of the ama ebi that come from the ocean. I think they just taste better.

Serves 4

You really don't have to do much to ama ebi to create a culinary hit. The flavor of its sweet meat comes out whether it's broiled, steamed, boiled, stir-fried, or barbecued. I've included three different dipping sauces, so take your pick, or use them all at once.

12 fresh large ama ebi
   (red-skinned shrimp)
Sauces for dipping: (your choice)
   Hijimi Rémoulade
   (see recipe below)

Wasabi Cocktail Sauce
   (see recipe below)
Spicy Citrus Dressing
   (see recipe below)

Steam ama ebi in a bamboo basket or perforated steamer for 5 to 7 minutes. Serve immediately with dipping sauce and lemon or lime wedges.

Garnish:

lemon or lime wedges

Hijimi Rémoulade:

1 cup mayonnaise
1 teaspoon hijimi
   (spicy Japanese pepper sprinkle)
1 teaspoon garlic, chopped
1 tablespoon green onion, chopped
1 teaspoon furikake (dried seaweed flakes)
1 teaspoon lemon juice
2 tablespoons water

Blend all ingredients.
Serve at room temperature.

Wasabi Cocktail Sauce:

1 tablespoon wasabi
   (Japanese horseradish paste)
1 teaspoon water
1/4 teaspoon Aloha shoyu
4 tablespoons ketchup
salt and pepper to taste

Blend all ingredients.

Spicy Citrus Dressing:

1/2 cup Aloha shoyu
1/2 cup cider vinegar
1/2 cup orange juice
2 tablespoons sesame oil
1/2 cup granulated sugar
1 teaspoon chili flakes
salt and pepper to taste

Mix ingredients together until sugar is dissolved.

Antique fishing net from Danny Akaka, Hawaiian Historian at the Mauna Lani Bay Hotel and Bungalows, Kohala Coast, Big Island; Oriental bamboo steamer provided by Nancy James, Host Marriott Corp., Polynesian Cultural Center, La'ie, O'ahu; sauce bowl by Georgio Sartoris.

'Ahi Tartare
with Ginger

Serves 4

The meat of the 'ahi oxidizes when exposed to air, and changes from a delicious red to a brown color in a matter of days. For this reason, the 'ahi is usually not filleted until shortly before use. Make sure to pick the freshest fish for this tartare appetizer.

Place heaping tablespoons of the tartare mixture in separate clumps on a bed of organic field greens, then lightly sprinkle black sesame seeds on the very top of each clump. To make it pretty, arrange edible flowers around the platter. It's a beautiful presentation. Really impressive.

1-1/2 pounds fresh 'ahi fillet
2 tablespoons sesame oil
2 tablespoons Mirin (Japanese
   sweet rice wine)

1 tablespoon rice vinegar
1/2 cup green onion, minced
1/2 tablespoon fresh ginger, minced
salt and pepper to taste

Mince the 'ahi with a very sharp knife. Place it in a glass or wooden bowl.

Add the sesame oil, Mirin, rice vinegar, green onions, and ginger. Mix well. Season with salt and pepper to taste. Refrigerate.

Garnish:

organic field greens
edible flowers
black goma (black sesame seeds)

Lomi Lomi Spooned 'O'io
(Bonefish)

Serves 4

This dish is a variation of Lomi Lomi Salmon. Garnish with chopped green onions, and serve very cold with poi. If you like, you can add a little sesame oil. It's unreal good.

1 pound whole 'o'io, raw
1 tablespoon Hawaiian salt,
   to sprinkle on 'o'io fillets
1/2 cup green onion
2 tablespoons 'inamona (roasted,
   ground and salted kukui nut meat)

1/2 cup limu kohu
1/2 cup limu ogo, chopped
2 small hot chilies, minced
2 cups salted ice water
1 to 2 cups fresh poi per person

'O'io, also known as "ladyfish" or "bonefish," is usually eaten raw. Once the fish is cooked, its many tiny bones, soft when raw, stiffen and make it complicated to eat. This fish is a favorite for use in Oriental fish cakes. In Hawai'i today, the meat is soaked in salted water for 3 to 4 hours, then scraped from the bones, and used in clear fish soup, or eaten as a seasoned mash.

Scale and clean the 'o'io, then split open from the back and butterfly. Sprinkle with Hawaiian salt, and refrigerate overnight. In the morning, scrape meat off the bones using a tablespoon. (Always scrape from head to tail.) Place fish meat in a large mixing bowl. Be sure there are no bones in the mixture. With a tablespoon, mix in other ingredients. Add water to thin mixture to desired consistency.

Garnish with chopped green onions, then serve with fresh poi.

Garnish:

1 tablespoon green onion, chopped

Seafood-Stuffed 'Opelu
with Tomato Lomi

Serves 4

This appetizer is easy to make, and it looks like it took lots of time. The nori wrap makes it appear kind of like sushi, but you add seafood stuffing with the dressing and lomi, and you've got a winner. Your guests are going to love you.

8 'opelu fillets, sliced 1/4-inch thin
Seafood Stuffing (see recipe below)
4 sheets nori (seaweed)
1/2 cup flour
2 eggs, for egg wash

3 cups panko (Japanese-style crispy bread crumbs)
1 cup vegetable oil for deep-frying
Tomato Lomi (see recipe below)
Spicy Citrus Dressing (see recipe below)

'Opelu was a very highly prized food in old Hawai'i. Its tender meat was eaten raw most of the time, but Hawaiians dried it and broiled it, too. The 'opelu from Waikiki and the Wai'anae coast were the best. They were fat. Lots of meat with very few bones.

Lay a piece of 'opelu, skin-side down on a flat surface. Place 1/4 seafood stuffing on the 'opelu; then place the other 'opelu fillet on top. The skin of 'opelu should be on the outside. Place on a sheet of nori, and roll. Repeat with the other fillets, making 4 stuffed 'opelu.

Place stuffed 'opelu in flour, then egg wash, and last, in the panko. Wrap them tightly in plastic wrap, and place in refrigerator for 1 hour to firm. Fry in oil at medium heat for 4 to 5 minutes. Slice, and serve with Tomato Lomi and Spicy Citrus Dressing on the side.

Seafood Stuffing:

2 tablespoons butter
1/4 cup round onion, minced
1/4 cup celery, minced
1/2 teaspoon garlic, minced
3/4 cup shrimp meat, chopped small
3/4 cup scallops, chopped small
1/4 cup crab meat, chopped small
   (imitation meat can be used)
1/2 teaspoon paprika
1/4 cup all-purpose flour
   1/4 cup heavy cream
      salt and pepper to taste

Heat butter in frying pan. Sauté onion, celery, and garlic. Add the seafood and paprika, and mix. Add flour, and blend. Last, pour in heavy cream, and cook for 3 to 5 minutes, stirring constantly. Add salt and pepper to taste.

Tomato Lomi:

1/2 medium onion, diced, about 1/4 inch
3 medium tomatoes, diced, about 1/4 inch
1/4 cup green onion, chopped
1 tablespoon cilantro, chopped
1/2 teaspoon garlic, minced
rock salt to taste
1/4 teaspoon chili flakes
juice of 1 lemon

Mix all ingredients together. Chill for 1 hour.

Spicy Citrus Dressing:

1/2 cup Aloha shoyu
1/2 cup cider vinegar
1/2 cup orange juice
2 tablespoons sesame oil
1/2 cup white sugar
1 teaspoon chili flakes
salt and pepper to taste

Mix ingredients together until sugar is dissolved.

Fabric background by Jan of Hina Lei Creations, Kamuela, Big Island; carvings by Dean Ka'ahanui of Ka'ahanui Kreations, Kamuela, Big Island; wooden platter provided by Georgia Sartoris of Georgia Sartoris Fine Art, Pa'auilo, Big Island.

"Catch of the Day"
Crispy Seafood Basket

Serves 12

This is a fun dish for any kind of gathering. It's pretty filling to eat alone, so make sure you have lots of friends to share it with.

Wasabi, the Japanese version of horseradish, has an extremely strong, sharp flavor that causes unsuspecting people to gasp for water. If you happen to get too much wasabi in one mouthful, don't drink water, eat rice. The sugars in the rice will comfort your burning mouth and throat.

1 pound scallops
2 pounds clams, shelled
1 pound shrimp, peeled and deveined
6 cups panko (Japanese-style crispy bread crumbs)
3 tablespoons fresh cilantro, minced

1-1/2 teaspoons whole celery seeds
1-1/2 teaspoons fresh thyme leaves
2-1/3 cups Tempura Batter (see recipe below)
Honey Wasabi Sauce (see recipe below)
salt and pepper to taste

Rinse scallops and clams in cold water. Drain well, and set aside with prepared shrimp.

Prepare Tempura Batter. Blend panko, cilantro, celery seeds, and thyme in a 2-inch-deep pan to make the breading. Dip seafood into Tempura Batter; coat well. Let excess drip off, then bread. Place breaded seafood onto parchment-lined sheetpans sprinkled with plain panko. Salt and pepper to taste. Cover and refrigerate. Make Honey Wasabi Sauce, and set aside.

Deep-fry seafood at 375° for 2 to 3 minutes until golden brown. Drain well on towels. Serve in parchment-lined basket with Honey Wasabi Sauce on the side.

Tempura Batter:

2 cups all-purpose flour
1 cup cornstarch
1 tablespoon baking powder
salt and pepper to taste
1-1/2 cups cold ale
1 raw egg

Combine dry ingredients, then add ale and egg. Whisk batter until smooth.

Honey Wasabi Sauce:

1 tablespoon wasabi (Japanese horseradish paste)
1/4 cup honey
1 cup mayonnaise
3 tablespoons sour cream
salt and pepper to taste

Combine all ingredients, and mix well. Set aside.

Breaded Oysters
with Wasabi Cocktail Sauce

Serves 4

Using the Pacific or Japanese oysters from the West Coast makes this appetizer perfect for people who aren't crazy about oysters. Their mild flavor fades a little more when they're breaded, and the wasabi sauce gets to show off its spicy punch. Pick any kind of oyster you like. It's a good idea to reserve the shells. You can place the breaded oysters back into the shells for an elegant presentation.

12 oysters
2/3 cup all-purpose flour
2 whole eggs, beaten
2-1/2 cups panko (Japanese-
   style crispy bread crumbs)

2 cups vegetable oil
Wasabi Cocktail Sauce
   (see recipe below)
salt and pepper to taste

To shuck an oyster, thrust the sturdy point of a knife between the shells under the small lip that sticks out near the hinge. Twist the knife to force the shell open. Once open, cut the muscle close to the top shell. Discard top shell. Use the knife to loosen the oyster from the bottom shell. Be careful not to cut yourself.

Coat oysters in flour, egg, then panko. Deep fry in oil at 350° until golden brown. Serve with Wasabi Cocktail Sauce.

Wasabi Cocktail Sauce

1-1/2 tablespoons wasabi
   (Japanese horseradish paste)
2 teaspoons water
2 teaspoons Aloha shoyu
1/2 cup ketchup
salt and pepper to taste

Mix ingredients together, and set aside.

Oyster shucker made by Dan DeLuz,
Dan DeLuz's Woods, Inc.

Ogo, Shrimp, & Scallop Tempura

Serves 4

Old Hawaiians have been using limu to dress up their seafood dishes for centuries. In fact, seafaring cultures all over the world, from Norway to Japan, have included seaweed in their diets since the beginning of time. Here in Hawai'i we've taken the name ogo from the Japanese to describe the limu we use in poke and other raw fish dishes.

This recipe is from an experiment with deep-frying. The only kind of limu or ogo that worked was long brown ogo. Its thin strands fry up into a crispy, mild-tasting coating over the chewy meat of tempura shrimp and scallops. It's a "broke da mouth" favorite in my restaurants.

8 pieces shrimp, 16-20 count per pound size
8 pieces sea scallops
8 ounces ogo (seaweed), thin, brown type

Tempura Batter (see recipe below)
Tempura Sauce (see recipe below)
vegetable oil for deep-frying
salt and pepper to taste

Prepare Tempura Batter, and set aside.

Heat oil to medium heat in wok. Dip seafood in Tempura Batter; then wrap in ogo. Salt and pepper to taste. Using a tong, hold ogo-breaded seafood in the hot oil for 10 seconds before releasing. Cook for 2 to 3 minutes, or until golden brown and crisp. Serve immediately with Tempura Sauce.

Tempura Batter:

1 cup all-purpose flour
1 cup cornstarch
1 tablespoon baking powder
1/4 teaspoon baking soda
1 large egg
1-1/2 cups cold water
salt and pepper to taste

Stir dry ingredients together. Place all liquids in a mixing bowl. Add the dry ingredients, salt, and pepper. Whip until all ingredients are combined, but still lumpy.

Tempura Sauce:

1 cup Aloha Shoyu
1/4 cup Mirin (Japanese sweet rice wine)
1 tablespoon rice vinegar
1 cup white sugar
1/2 cup water
2 slices ginger

Place all ingredients in a saucepan, and simmer for 20 minutes. Serve warm.

Ceramic appetizer platter by artist Kyle Ino of Kane'ohe, O'ahu; dipping saucer by Betsi Kohler of Betsi's Bowls of Volcano, Big Island; foliage donated by Eric S. Tanouye of Green Point Nursery, Hilo, Big Island; ogo provided by Steven A. Katase of Royal Hawaiian Sea Farms, Kailua-Kona, Big Island.

ECCO DOMANI.
ITALIAN RED WINE

— 1996 —
MERLOT
DELLE
VENEZIE
INDICAZIONE GEOGRAFICA TIPICA
IMPORTED BY ECCO DOMANI USA, INC., SANTA ROSA CA, ALC. 12% BY VOL.

Chinese Scallops
with Chili-Ginger Oil and Black Beans

Serves 4

Sea scallops, the largest commercial scallop sold in the United
States, are collected year round
in the Atlantic, from the Labrador
Coast to New Jersey, in waters up
to 900 feet deep. Peak harvest
season is during the months of
March through November.

The hot, spicy Chili-Ginger Oil really brings out the flavor of these large scallops. The stir-fried vegetables and black beans give the dish a real Chinese flare.
And as a bonus, it is a really colorful dish that tastes as good as it looks.

Scallops:
1 pound sea scallops
2 tablespoons peanut oil
1/2 cup fresh ginger, peeled
  and thinly sliced

3 tablespoons preserved black beans
1/2 large red bell pepper, julienned
1/2 large yellow bell pepper, julienned
salt and pepper to taste
Chili-Ginger Oil (see recipe below)

Heat the peanut oil in a wok over moderate heat. Add the ginger and scallops.
Cook for 2 minutes, stirring constantly. Add the black beans and bell peppers.
Cook for 1 minute more, stirring constantly. Add salt and pepper to taste.
Remove the scallops from heat, and arrange on fresh spinach leaves. Drizzle
with the Chili-Ginger Oil. Serve immediately.

Chili-Ginger Oil:

1/2 cup peanut oil
4 fresh Hawaiian chili peppers
1/2 cup fresh ginger, peeled and minced
2 cloves fresh garlic, sliced thin
2 tablespoons sesame oil
2 tablespoons Aloha shoyu

Heat the peanut oil in a wok over moderate
heat. Add the chilies, ginger, and garlic. Stir
constantly for 2 minutes. It will sizzle. Add the
sesame oil and shoyu, and cook for 2 minutes
more. Remove from heat, cool slightly, and
strain. Set aside.

Garnish:

2 cups fresh spinach leaves

Deep-Fried Crab Meat Balls
with Sweet & Sour Pineapple Sauce

Serves 4-6

Drizzle the Sweet & Sour Pineapple Sauce over the crab meat balls in a thin stream. That way the sweet/sour flavor doesn't overwhelm the delicate taste of the meat. We've offered this dish at some of my restaurants, and it never fails. It's always a favorite.

1 pound lump crab meat
1 egg
1 tablespoon sherry
3 tablespoons scallion, minced
1 pound fresh shiitake mushrooms, minced
1 tablespoon fresh cilantro, minced
1 tablespoon oyster sauce
2 tablespoons mayonnaise

1 cup bread crumbs
salt and white pepper to taste
1 egg, for egg wash
2 teaspoons water
2 cups cornstarch, for dredging
vegetable oil, for deep frying (use your discretion)
Sweet & Sour Pineapple Sauce (see recipe below)

Pick over crab meat. Then mince, and combine all other ingredients in a large bowl. Mix well. Shape mixture into balls, 1-inch diameter, and set aside.

Prepare egg wash by whipping egg with 2 teaspoons of water. Dip crab balls into egg wash, then into cornstarch. Deep-fry to a golden brown.

Drain on a paper towel. Great when served over a bed of shredded cabbage and topped with my famous Sweet & Sour Pineapple Sauce.

Canned crab meat, commercially sold in Hawai'i in 6- to 8-ounce cans, is pasteurized and heat-sealed to protect it from contamination. It's sometimes a little watery from the can, so make sure to drain it before using. You can also get imitation crab meat. It's not my favorite, but it can be used in all of the crab meat recipes in this book.

GOSSAMER BAY
VINEYARDS
CALIFORNIA
SAUVIGNON BLANC
1995

Sweet & Sour Pineapple Sauce:

3/4 cup pineapple juice
1 cup brown sugar
1 cup white wine vinegar
1 tablespoon Aloha shoyu
1 tablespoon ketchup
2 slices of fresh ginger
1 tablespoon cornstarch and 1/4 cup water, for thickening.

Bring pineapple juice to a boil. Add sugar, and cook until sugar is dissolved. Add the vinegar, shoyu, ketchup, and ginger to mixture, and boil for about 3 to 4 minutes. Make a cornstarch mixture by blending 1 tablespoon cornstarch with 1/4 cup water. Add cornstarch mixture to sauce, and cook until thickened. Set aside.

Garnish:

2 cups cabbage, shredded

Oyster Cakes
with Hijimi Rémoulade

Serves 4

Old Hawaiians called most shellfish "pupu," meaning small sea or land shells. The old folks decided to call appetizers "pupus" (little bits of food) because that's all that would fit in the little shells.

3 cups panko (Japanese-style
   crispy bread crumbs)
1/4 cup cilantro, chopped
salt and pepper to taste
16 large oysters

3/4 cup all-purpose flour
3 large eggs, beaten
1-1/2 cups vegetable oil
Hijimi Rémoulade (see recipe below)

Combine panko with cilantro and a little salt and pepper.

Dredge oysters in flour, dip in eggs, and coat with panko mixture.

In a large skillet, heat oil to medium-high temperature. Deep-fry oysters 1-1/2 to 2 minutes on each side, until golden brown. Serve with Hijimi Rémoulade.

Hijimi Rémoulade:

1 cup mayonnaise
1 teaspoon hijimi (spicy Japanese
   pepper sprinkle)
1 teaspoon garlic, chopped
1 tablespoon green onion, chopped
1 teaspoon furikake (dried seaweed flakes)
1 teaspoon lemon juice
2 tablespoons water

Blend all ingredients.
Serve at room temperature.

SONOMA RESERVE
TURNING LEAF
SONOMA COUNTY
CHARDONNAY
1994

Fabric design by Junko Week; plate provided by Liberty House; dipping dish by Betsi Kohler of Betsi's Bowls in Volcano on the Big Island; and flowers by Eric S. Tanouye of Green Point Nursery in Hilo, Big Island, and Kelvin T. Sewake, Hilo, Big Island.

Island-Style Stir-Fried Shrimp

Serves 6-8

Most shrimp come to Hawai'i frozen or previously frozen. To give us the freshest possible product, shrimp are frozen right after harvest. Be careful, though. Some shrimp from the Mainland that are sold "fresh," and have never been frozen, are treated with sulfites to prevent discoloration. This kind of preservative sometimes triggers allergic reactions in people with asthma.

This is an easy dish to make on the spur of the moment, if you have some hefty shrimp on hand. Lightly seasoned, this dish is great hot or cold. It makes the perfect "munchy" for Sunday afternoons on the lanai, or tailgating in the parking lot, waiting for the stadium gates to open.

1 pound shrimp, peeled and deveined
2 tablespoons Aloha shoyu
1 tablespoon dry sherry
1 tablespoon fresh ginger, minced
1 green onion, minced

1/2 teaspoon salt
3 tablespoons peanut oil
1 teaspoon granulated sugar

Rinse shrimp, leave whole. Combine shoyu, sherry, ginger, green onion, and salt. Blend well, and set aside.

Heat wok or skillet; add oil. Add shrimp, and stir-fry until pinkish, about 1 to 2 minutes. Sprinkle with sugar, and stir-fry 1/2 minute more. Add shoyu mixture, and cook 2 minutes more. Serve hot or cold.

Lobster Boil
with Hawaiian Salt, Chili Peppers & Other Stuffs

Serves 4

Be careful not to overcook the lobster. You run the risk of tough and rubbery meat if you cook it too long. Slice the lobster meat into bite-size pieces as soon as it is cooked. Spread the cooked vegetables over the bottom of a serving dish, then place the meat in the center. Drizzle some of the reserved cooking wine over the top, and you're set for a real treat.

1 whole lobster
1 or 2 red chili peppers, crushed
1 carrot, coarsely chopped
1 onion, coarsely chopped
1 tablespoon fresh cilantro, chopped

1 tablespoon cracked peppercorns
2 tablespoons white wine
3 cups water
pinch of Hawaiian salt
1 lemon, cut into quarters

When I was younger, I went lobster fishing with the older men. There was a place where the lobsters were so thick—their antennae and feelers sticking out all over the place—it looked like a nest of bugs. That's what we called them, "bugs." It's really spooky to see when you're night fishing. My favorite way to eat lobsters is boiled. It's the easiest way to cook them, and it doesn't hide any of the great flavor.

In a large wok, bring all ingredients (except lobster) to a boil.

Add lobster, and cover. Cook about 10 to 15 minutes, until lobster is just cooked.

Fresh Oysters
w/Jicama and Fresh Chili Lime Shoyu

Serves 4

There are three primary types of oysters grown commercially on the Mainland—the Eastern, Pacific, and tiny Olympic. Eastern oysters are found in bays and inlets stretching from Canada to the Carolinas. Pacific or Japanese oysters come from farms in California, Oregon, southeast Alaska, and Washington. Olympics are raised off the shores of the Olympic Peninsula in Washington state.

This is one of my favorite appetizer recipes. It's great. The tangy-hot flavor of shoyu and chili pepper really complements the salty oyster taste. You add the texture difference of crunchy jicama (Chinese yam) and tender oysters, drizzle with a little lime juice, and you've got a mouth-puckering treat. 'Ono-licious!

1/3 cup Aloha shoyu
1 Hawaiian chili pepper, minced
16 pieces oyster meat

2 limes, cut into wedges
16 jicama (Chinese yam),
   1/2-inch diced

Mix shoyu with Hawaiian chili pepper. Divide oyster meat and shoyu/chili sauce into 4 shooter glasses.

Skewer lime wedge and 1/2-inch diced jicama with a wooden toothpick. Place in shooter glasses.

Shooter glasses by glass etcher Gary Wagner; nautical brass porthole provided by Mary & Captain Mike Remer of Mariner's Canteen; painted wooden fish provided by Nancy James of Host Marriott's Shop Polynesia at the Polynesian Cultural Center.

Oysters on the Half-Shell
with Ginger Daikon Sauce

Serves 1-2

I love oysters on the half-shell. They look all dressed up without any work, and you really get to taste the full flavor. I like to add a little dab of pesto and some ginger/daikon to bring out the taste even more. Try it, I think you'll like it, too.

6 oysters on the half-shell

1/2 cup Ginger Daikon Sauce (see recipe below)

In a deep platter, arrange oysters in a circle on a bed of ice. Top each oyster with a dab of Ginger Pesto. Place a small cup of Ginger Daikon Sauce in the middle, and serve.

Ginger Daikon Sauce:

2 tablespoons Ginger Pesto
  (see recipe)
2 tablespoons daikon (white turnip),
  finely grated
1 tablespoon Aloha shoyu

Blend.

Ginger Pesto:

1 cup light olive oil
1 teaspoon salt
1/4 cup fresh ginger, minced
1/2 cup green onion, minced
1/4 cup fresh cilantro, minced
  and lightly packed
1/8 teaspoon white pepper

Combine all ingredients to make the pesto.

Steamed Clams and Shrimp
with Spicy Black Beans

Serves 6

This is what I like to do—I arrange the shrimp and clams on a mound of steamed rice. Put the platter in the middle of the living room table during a football game. Give your guests chopsticks, then sit back and watch them go at it. I'm never surprised when I have to make another batch before the half.

1 teaspoon fresh ginger, minced
3 tablespoons scallion, minced
1 teaspoon brown sugar
2 tablespoons black beans
1 teaspoon pepper flakes
1 tablespoon olive oil

1 pound shrimp (21 to 25),
  peeled and deveined
24 clams
1 tablespoon sherry
1 tablespoon Aloha shoyu
salt and white pepper to taste

In some of my recipes I've included the number of shrimp per pound to give you an idea of the size that works best (example: 21 to 25 pieces per pound). In United States markets shrimp are sold and priced according to size—the bigger they are, the fewer you get and the more they cost per pound. Shrimp come really little, from the tiny "salad" shrimp, with 70 to 90 shrimp per pound, to the largest "colossal" shrimp, with less than 10 per pound.

In a large bowl, mix ginger, scallions, brown sugar, black beans, pepper flakes, and olive oil into a paste.

Arrange shrimp and clams in a steamer pot. Drizzle the black bean mixture over top of shellfish. Steam for about 10 to 12 minutes. Remove liquid, add the sherry and shoyu, and thicken with Cornstarch Mixture. Place steamed clams and shrimp on serving platter, and pour black bean sauce over the top.

Cornstarch Mixture:

2 tablespoons cornstarch
1 tablespoon water

Always, when adding cornstarch mixture as a thickening agent, be sure to bring the liquid to a boil before adding the constarch mixture. Stir constantly, and cook for about 1 to 2 minutes.

'Ahi Cakes
with Wasabi Aioli

Serves 2

You can use these 'ahi cakes in a number of ways once they're cooked. They are wonderful in a sandwich, served as finger food at a party, or the topping for a cool summer salad.

In old Hawai'i, food that couldn't be consumed in one sitting was dried. 'Ahi was cut into 6-inch long steaks, sprinkled with salt, placed into a container (lauhala basket or umeke or calabash) that was filled with salt. After three days, the meat was taken out, rinsed, and set on flat beach stones to dry in the sun.

1 (8 ounce) 'ahi fillet, minced
2 tablespoons mayonnaise
1 tablespoon green onion, chopped
1 tablespoon ogo, chopped
1 tablespoon Aloha shoyu
1 teaspoon sesame oil

2 tablespoons panko (Japanese-style crispy bread crumbs)
2 teaspoons fresh dill, chopped
2 tablespoons all-purpose flour, for dipping
2 tablespoons light olive oil
1 cup Wasabi Aioli (see recipe below)

Mix 'ahi, mayonnaise, green onions, ogo, shoyu, sesame oil, panko, and dill. Form 4 small cakes. Dust with flour. Heat olive oil in pan, and cook cakes about 2 minutes on each side, until golden brown. Place on a platter garnished with salad greens, and drizzle with Wasabi Aioli.

Wasabi Aioli:

2 tablespoons wasabi
  (Japanese horseradish paste)
1 cup mayonnaise
1 tablespoon light olive oil
salt and pepper to taste

Whisk all ingredients together. Set aside.

Garnish:

1 cup mixed salad greens

Furikake-Crusted Sashimi

Serves 4

I like to marinate, then sear the fish quickly to lock in the flavors. The bright red center of the meat and the seared, brown edges combine for a beautiful presentation.

1 tablespoon wasabi
   (Japanese horseradish paste)
2 tablespoons Aloha shoyu
2 'ahi (yellowfin tuna) or
   swordfish fillets, 1 pound each

1/4 cup furikake (dried seaweed flakes)
cooking spray
Sweet-and-Sour Cucumber
   Vinaigrette (see recipe below)

Sashimi, thinly sliced, bite-sized pieces of raw fish, are a big part of Hawai'i's local culinary landscape. Brought in by Japanese immigrants to the Islands, this simple dish has crossed all cultural boundaries, and is served throughout the state at parties, neighborhood gatherings, office functions, and everywhere people are having a great time.

In a small bowl, combine wasabi and shoyu. Marinate fish in shoyu mixture for 30 minutes. Roll fillets in furikake to crust. Coat hot pan with cooking spray, and quickly sear fish about 15 to 30 seconds. Slice sashimi-style (in thin, 2-by-2-by-1/4-inch slices).

Arrange sashimi on a bed of fresh organic field greens, and drizzle with Sweet-and-Sour Cucumber Vinaigrette.

Sweet-and-Sour Cucumber Vinaigrette

1 cup white vinegar
1/2 cup water
3/4 cup granulated sugar
pinch of salt
1 cup cucumbers, grated
1/2 tablespoon ginger, grated

Blend until sugar dissolves. Chill.

Garnish:

fresh organic field greens

SOUPS & SALADS

Deep-Sea Fishing

I think my favorite kind of fishing nowadays is deep-sea fishing. From the art of the lures to the thrill of sailing out on a fast sport-fishing boat, to the excitement of reeling in a fighting marlin, it's the best.

I've learned, over the years, how important the lures are, and how much fishing lore and story go into making them. For good reason the lure makers are proud of their craft. They listen to the fishermen—or go out fishing themselves—and take notice of the colors that attract certain fish, or how the trailing ends are cut to produce a streak of irresistable foam.

'Ahi prefer purple, blue, and silver, and smaller beads on the lure. Marlin go after purple and black. Pinks and reds pull in mahimahi. But, really, the colors and shapes of the lures—and the lure makers know this—catch the fishermen first, then the fish. You go into the fishing supply store and you buy lures that look pretty. They catch your eye. You buy.

The ones you keep, though, are the ones that work. I have a box of lures at home, and I remember some of the great fish I've caught with them.

The good lures have stories. "This is the one that caught a 1,500-pound marlin due west of Kailua-Kona; this one hooked three huge 'ahi in one day." Like that.

There are tricks to finding the fish, and the best lures won't help unless you know where to troll. Searching for fish you have to look at currents and tides, the temperature of the water. You scan the horizon for "bird piles," which are seabirds stacked up over a swarm of bait fish, the filefish, baby flying fish, shrimp. That's where the big fish are running.

You go and put your hooks out where the birds are, and start trolling. And if you're lucky, there's a strike. The reel spins with that great sound, half scream, half song. And you know you've got a big one.

Then it's Chinese fire drill, everyone scrambling to help land the monster that's pulling so strong. Whoever is in the fighting chair is assisted in whatever way—someone helping to hand-line the fish in, everyone else shouting encouragement. There's nothing like landing a huge marlin, or a quick-darting mahimahi, or a beautiful, fiery 'ahi. Fishing for the biggest fish in the Pacific Ocean is the greatest thrill a fisherman could hope for.

Dungeness Crab Soup

Serves 6

You can substitute any type of crab meat in this soup, but I highly recommend using the sweet meat of the giant Dungeness crab. Serve it with garlic croutons, or large pieces of garlic sourdough toast.

2 tablespoons sweet butter	1/3 cup tomato paste
1/4 cup celery, diced	2-1/2 cups chicken stock
1/4 cup carrots, diced	1 cup clam juice
2 tablespoons green onion, minced	salt and pepper to taste
1 teaspoon fresh garlic, minced	1/4 cup heavy cream
1/4 cup all-purpose flour	8 ounces Dungeness crab meat

Melt the butter, and sauté celery, carrots, green onion, garlic, and flour for about 3 to 4 minutes. Add tomato paste. Cook for 10 minutes, stirring constantly. Add chicken stock and clam juice. Bring to a boil, then reduce heat and simmer for 45 minutes. Add salt and pepper to taste. Fold in heavy cream and Dungeness crab meat.

Dungeness crabs are sold whole in hard shells, as pasteurized claws, as crab meat that has been removed from the shell, and as fully cooked and frozen claws or legs. Any one of these preparations will work perfectly in this soup.

GOSSAMER BAY
V I N E Y A R D S
CALIFORNIA
SAUVIGNON BLANC
1995

'Ahi Salad
with Creamy Peanut Dressing

Serves 4

On one of my trips, I got to taste this incredible Thai peanut dressing. I came home and put together this recipe. It's a little bit Thai, a little bit Chinese, and a lot wild, with the won bok and red cabbage, bean sprouts and mushrooms. All the more reason to try it.

In Hawai'i, the yellowfin tuna is also called by its Japanese name "shibi." Old Hawaiians gave the 'ahi its name because of the bright yellow color of its soft dorsal and anal fins. When large schools swam under the canoes, they gave the illusion of yellow flames streaking through the water.

2 cups won bok (Chinese cabbage), shredded
1-1/2 cups fresh mushrooms, sliced
1-1/2 cups fresh bean sprouts
3/4 cup radishes, slivered
1 cup red cabbage, shredded
1/2 cup green onion, chopped
1 large tomato, cut into 12 wedges
1/2 pound 'ahi (yellowfin tuna), cubed and seared
salt and pepper to taste
Creamy Peanut Dressing (see recipe below)

Toss together won bok, mushrooms, bean sprouts, radishes, cabbage, green onion, and tomatoes. Place seared 'ahi on top of the greens. Add salt and pepper to taste. Garnish with fresh cilantro and chopped peanuts. Serve with Creamy Peanut Dressing on the side.

Garnish:

fresh cilantro, minced
peanuts, finely chopped

Creamy Peanut Dressing:
1/2 cup warm water
1/2 cup creamy peanut butter
1-1/2 tablespoons rice vinegar
2 tablespoons Aloha shoyu
1/4 cup granulated sugar
1/2 teaspoon salt
1 clove fresh garlic, crushed
1/4 cup salad oil
1-1/2 teaspoons sambal oelek (chili paste)
2 tablespoons fresh cilantro, minced

Mix water and peanut butter in a small bowl, until smooth. Add remaining dressing ingredients, and mix well. Let stand at room temperature at least 30 minutes.

Glass platter lent by Liz Hersage of Prestige Designs Hawai'i, Kamuela, Big Island; oyster mushrooms, donated by Kona Mushrooms Inc., Kailua-Kona, Big Island; fish chopstick holders lent by Jeane Nakahara of Antique Sakae, Hilo, Big Island; chopsticks by John S. Pierl, lent by Volcano Art Gallery, Hawai'i National Park, Big Island; small sauce bowl made by artist Georgia Sartoris of Georgia Sartoris Fine Art, Pa'auilo, Big Island.

Baby Romaine Lettuce
with Honey Ginger Bay Scallops & Fresh Bay Shrimp

Serves 4-6

The mild and sweet bay scallops are considered the best-testing of all scallops. The flesh is lean and firm, but delicate. Bay scallops range in color from ivory to pink to light apricot, and the meat averages 1/2 to 3/4-inch in thickness.

ECCO DOMANI
ITALIAN WHITE WINE
1996
PINOT GRIGIO
DELLE
VENEZIE
INDICAZIONE GEOGRAFICA TIPICA
IMPORTED BY ECCO DOMANI USA, INC, SANTA ROSA CA, ALC. 12% BY VOL.

The tiny shellfish in this recipe add a delicate, but powerful flavor to the salad. To serve it up right, drizzle with a Ginger Pesto, and scatter it on a bed of baby romaine lettuce. It's a real pleaser.

1 cup bay shrimp
1 cup bay scallops
2 tablespoons honey
juice from 1 fresh lime

1 tablespoon Ginger Pesto
 (see recipe below)
salt and pepper to taste
1 tablespoon vegetable oil,
 for frying

Marinate shrimp and scallops in honey, lime juice, pesto, salt, and pepper for about 5 minutes. Heat oil in a wok until smoking, then add shrimp and scallops. Cook until just done—about 2 minutes. Pour over lettuce.

Ginger Pesto:

1 cup light olive oil
1 teaspoon salt
1/4 cup fresh ginger, minced
1/4 cup green onion, minced
1/4 cup fresh cilantro, minced,
 lightly packed
1/8 teaspoon white pepper

Combine all ingredients to make the pesto, and set aside.

Garnish:

4 heads baby romaine lettuce

THE CHOY OF SEAFOOD | SOUPS & SALADS

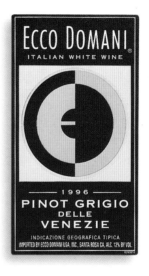

Garnish:

4 heads baby romaine lettuce

Spicy Soy Shrimp Salad

Serves 4

To make this a little more fancy, you can serve it in a deep-fried flour tortilla basket instead of using the tortilla wedges described below. Topped with butterflied shrimp, tomato wedges, and cucumber slices, and garnished with cilantro leaves, it's a beautiful dish either way.

These fine Japanese noodles are usually produced from hard wheat flour mixed with oil. Most somen are white, but you'll sometimes see a yellow variety that contains egg yolk. Stored in a cool, dry place, dried somen will keep almost indefinitely.

20 pieces shrimp (16-20 pieces per
   pound), butterflied with shells on
Marinade (see recipe below)
1 pound mixed tossed greens
1 package somen noodles, cooked
12 tomato wedges

12 cucumber slices
4 (6-inch) flour tortillas, each cut
   into 8 wedges, and deep-fried
Sam Choy's Original Oriental
   Creamy Dressing (see recipe below)

Marinate shrimp for 1/2 hour. Heat oil in a wok. Stir-fry marinated shrimp for 1 minute. Remove from heat.

Divide tossed greens onto four large plates, top with somen, and shrimp. Arrange 3 tomato wedges and 3 cucumber slices on each plate. Sprinkle with crispy flour tortilla wedges, and garnish with cilantro leaves. Serve with Sam Choy's Original Oriental Creamy Dressing.

Marinade:

1/4 cup Aloha shoyu
1 teaspoon fresh garlic, chopped
1 teaspoon fresh cilantro, chopped
1 teaspoon chili sauce
1 teaspoon green onion, chopped
1 tablespoon granulated sugar
1 tablespoon sesame oil
1 teaspoon sesame seeds, roasted

Mix all ingredients together, and set aside.

Garnish:

cilantro leaves

**Sam Choy's Original Oriental
Creamy Dressing:**

3 cups mayonnaise
1/2 cup Aloha shoyu
3/4 cup granulated sugar
1/4 teaspoon white pepper
1-1/2 tablespoons black goma (black
   sesame seeds)
1 tablespoon sesame oil
2 tablespoons water

Whisk all ingredients together until well blended.

Seafood Cream of Broccoli Soup

Serves 4

This is a hearty, "stick-to-the-ribs" soup for those cold, rainy-season nights when you wish you had a fireplace. Serve local-style with sweet bread or taro rolls. There's no garnish or fanfare needed, just bring it to the table. It makes a basic, very satisfying, earthy meal.

3/4 cup ono (wahoo), cubed
3/4 cup shrimp, diced
1/2 cup crab meat, diced
1 medium onion, diced
3/4 cup celery, diced
1 teaspoon garlic, minced
6 tablespoons butter

4 cups broccoli, stems and flowers, chopped
1/2 cup all-purpose flour
8 cups chicken broth
1 cup cream
salt and pepper to taste

In a pot, cook the seafood—ono, shrimp, and crab meat—in chicken broth for 4 to 5 minutes. Separate the broth from the seafood, and set aside.

In the soup pot, sauté onions, celery, and garlic in butter, until onions are translucent. Add broccoli, and cook until broccoli is soft. Stir in flour, and mix well. Add reserved broth slowly, blend well, and simmer for 25 minutes. Add the cream, then salt and pepper to taste. Simmer for 15 minutes more. Purée and strain. Fold in cooked seafood, and serve hot.

As a seasonal substitution, restaurants often use ono instead of mahimahi. In most cases, the texture and flavor of these two fish are interchangeable, although the mahimahi is usually the more moist and sweeter of the two. Because ono tends to dry out quickly, cooking techniques used for "lean" fish with low fat content are best. Poaching works very well.

GOSSAMER BAY
VINEYARDS

CALIFORNIA
SAUVIGNON BLANC
1995

ALC. 11.5% BY VOL. 62280F

Soup bowl provided by Liberty House, Honolulu, O'ahu; green fabric napkin lent by Brenda Schott and Kimo of Under the Koa Tree, Waikoloa Resort, Big Island; koa bread board lent by Makana O Hawaii Gift Shop and made by Maika'i Wood Hawaii, Mauna Lani Bay Hotel and Bungalows, Big Island; flowers donated by Roen Hufford and Marie McDonald, Kamuela, Big Island; bread rolls donated by Renee Dyer, Kailua-Kona, Big Island.

Poached Scallops
with a Tarragon Vinaigrette

Serves 6

Scallops are a bivalve mollusk (animal with a two-piece shell around its soft, boneless body). Most live in shallow waters, but some can be found at depths of 4-1/2 miles. While on a pilgrimage (journey to a holy place), people of the Middle Ages wore scallop shells on their hats.

I divided the ingredient list into three sections, each one contributing a different element to the salad. The first is for the scallops, the second is for the marinade, and the third is for the salad base. This is perfect for a hot summer evening while you're watching the horizon for the "green flash."

1-1/2 pounds bay scallops
1-1/2 cups water
3 tablespoons fresh lemon juice
1/2 teaspoon salt
3 black peppercorns
3 slices Maui (sweet) onion

6 servings Waimea Mixed Salad
  Greens
3/4 cup red radish, sliced
2 medium tomatoes, cut into wedges
1 Asian apple, julienned
1 jicama (Chinese yam), julienned

1/3 cup tarragon vinegar
2/3 cup light olive oil
1/3 cup granulated sugar
1 clove fresh garlic, sliced
1 teaspoon salt
1-1/2 cups celery, sliced diagonally

Rinse scallops with cold water, and drain well. Combine 1-1/2 cups water, lemon juice, 1/2 teaspoon salt, peppercorns, and onion slices in a saucepan, and bring to a boil. Add scallops, reduce heat, and simmer for 3 to 5 minutes, or until scallops are tender. Drain scallops.

Combine vinegar, oil, sugar, garlic, and the 1 teaspoon salt. Stir until sugar is dissolved. Pour over scallops, cover, and chill for several hours.

Add celery to scallops, and mix. Drain, but save marinade.

Arrange mixed greens evenly on six salad plates. Divide scallops and celery mixture evenly among the six plates. Arrange the remaining ingredients in groups around the scallops on a bed of the mixed greens. Drizzle reserved marinade over each of the six scallop salads.

Etched green platter made by Jennifer Pontz of Tropical Art Glass, Holualoa, Big Island; flowers donated by Amy and Mike Rosato, Island Orchids, Kailua-Kona, Big Island.

Cold Shrimp
and Long Rice Salad

Serves 4

Kamaboko is a Japanese fish paste that consists of puréed white fish mixed with potato starch and salt, then steamed. Kamaboko is ready to eat straight from the package; you'll find it in logs, cakes, and loaves, sometimes tinted bright pink around the edges.

I love working with long rice. It has a very interesting taste and texture, and it works well in salads. Besides, it's just really fun to eat. It's sometimes too fragile to roll around the tongs of a fork, and you have to kind of slurp it up.

1 package (2 ounces) long rice
20 medium shrimp, cooked
  and peeled
1 medium-size won bok
  (Chinese cabbage), thinly sliced
1 red and white kamaboko
  (fish cake), thinly sliced

1/2 cup carrots, grated
2 eggs, fried and thinly sliced
1 medium chili pepper, sliced
salt and pepper to taste
Long Rice Salad Dressing
  (see recipe below)

Pour hot water over long rice. Let stand about 20 minutes, then drain.

Combine all ingredients for the salad. Toss with dressing, season with salt and pepper, and chill for 1 to 2 hours. Before serving, garnish with watercress.

Garnish:

1/2 bunch fresh watercress,
  cut 2 inches long

Long Rice Salad Dressing:

1/2 cup granulated sugar
1/2 cup apple cider vinegar
1/2 cup sesame oil
1/2 cup Aloha shoyu

Mix together, and set aside.

Wok-Fried Red Lettuce and Red Oak
with Ginger Slivers, Garlic & Fried Shrimp

Serves 4

The slightly wilted lettuces blended deliciously into this dish make for an interesting texture—half salad, half soup. The furikake and black goma add a truly Oriental flavor, while the tequila-marinated shrimp pushes it over the top.

1 tablespoon vegetable oil
1 head red leaf lettuce
1 head red oak lettuce
1 tablespoon fresh ginger,
  cut in fine slivers
1 tablespoon fresh garlic, minced
Hawaiian salt
1/4 cup chicken stock

1 tablespoon furikake (dried
  seaweed flakes)
1 tablespoon black goma (black
  sesame seeds)
1 tablespoon green onion, chopped
Batterless Wok-Fried Shrimp
  (see recipe below)

Wilted salads are very popular. Just be sure to cut or chop your greens into pieces that are easy to handle. I like to cut them into 1-1/2-inch thick strips. They are big enough to allow the texture to come through, and small enough to manage with a fork.

Heat oil in a wok until smoking. Add lettuce, ginger, garlic, salt, then chicken stock. Cook about 1 minute, until lettuce is wilted. Place in a bowl. Sprinkle with furikake, black goma, and green onion, top with Batterless Wok-Fried Shrimp.

Batterless Wok-Fried Shrimp:

1 pound shrimp, peeled and deveined
  (21-25 count per pound)
2 tablespoons tequila
1 teaspoon fresh garlic, minced
1 teaspoon granulated sugar
1/2 teaspoon salt
2 tablespoons oil for frying
4 tablespoons Aloha shoyu

Place shrimp in a bowl, sprinkle with tequila and salt, and toss. Let marinate for 10 to 15 minutes, tossing occasionally. Drain off excess liquid. Meanwhile, heat oil in wok. BE CAREFUL, the oil will be sizzling and very hot. Add shrimp, and cook for 3 to 4 minutes. Add remaining ingredients, let simmer for another 2 to 3 minutes. Remove shrimp.

Maui Fisherman's Soup

Serves 4

Here's a hearty soup. A good soup. Originated by men of the sea who knew how best to serve up their catch.

6 cups chicken broth

2 large stalks of lemon grass, with tough outer leaves discarded, and lower stalk trimmed to 12 inches and angle-cut into 2-inch pieces

3 large slices unpeeled fresh ginger, about 2 ounces

1 can (14 ounces) unsweetened coconut milk

3 teaspoons Chili-Tamarind Paste (available in Asian supermarkets)

1/4 cup fresh lemon juice

1/4 cup brown sugar

1/4 cup Thai Fish Sauce (available in Asian supermarkets)

8 fresh New Zealand green tip mussels

8 medium-size scallops

8 medium shrimp, deveined, peeled, and butterflied

2 small fresh Thai Chilies or chili peppers, stemmed and lightly crushed

Put the broth, lemon grass, and ginger in a soup pot. Gradually bring to a boil over medium-high heat. Boil for 1 minute. Stir in the coconut milk, and return to a boil. Add the Chili-Tamarind Paste, lemon juice, sugar, and fish sauce. Stir until the paste and sugar are dissolved and blended. Reduce the heat, and simmer gently while you prepare the mussels.

Return the soup to a boil. Add the mussels, scallops, and shrimp. Do not stir. Bring back to a boil for about 1 minute. Float the chilies on top, and turn off the heat. Ladle the soup into a steamboat, a soup tureen, or individual serving bowls. Tear a sprig or two of cilantro over each serving.

Garnish:

Sprigs of fresh cilantro

To prepare mussels, agitate the water in which the mussels are soaking. (Live mussels open and close to breathe. Any mussels that don't eventually close are dead, and should be discarded.) Scrub and debeard the mussels. After cooking, drain and let cool. Gently pry the mussels open, breaking them apart at the hinge ends. Discard the upper shells, reserving the mussels on their half shells.

Indigo Hills
1995
North Coast
SAUVIGNON BLANC

Bowl by Ronald Hanatani of RYH Pottery, Volcano, Big Island; starfish lent by Nancy James of Host/Marriott, Polynesian Cultural Center, La'ie, O'ahu; shells provided by Pi'i Laeha, Laupahoehoe, Big Island; fabric donated by Mamo Howell, Inc., Honolulu, O'ahu.

Macadamia Nut-Crusted Ono Caesar Salad

Serves 4

Another name for ono is wahoo. When European explorers first arrived in Hawai'i, they found vast numbers of ono off the shores of the island of O'ahu. Trying to translate Hawaiian words into English spelling was difficult, and on their maps they spelled O'ahu, "Wahoo." They were so impressed by the thick population of ono in the area, that they named the fish "wahoo" as well.

Caesar salad can be a meal all by itself. To serve this salad, place romaine lettuce leaves in a salad bowl, and toss with dressing. Divide the lettuce among the four plates, place one fish fillet atop each salad, and garnish with freshly ground black pepper, croutons, and Parmesan cheese.

2 medium heads romaine lettuce,
   washed, dried, and torn
Caesar Salad Dressing
   (see recipe below)

2 Macadamia Nut-Crusted Ono
   (wahoo) (see recipe below)

Garnish:

croutons
1/4 cup Parmesan cheese,
   freshly grated
freshly ground black pepper to taste

Caesar Salad Dressing:

1 egg yolk
1 tablespoon Dijon mustard
1 teaspoon fresh lemon juice
2 cloves fresh garlic, minced
1 tablespoon anchovies, minced
dash Tabasco sauce
2 teaspoons Worcestershire sauce
2 tablespoons red wine vinegar
2 tablespoons Parmesan cheese
1/4 cup water
salt and pepper to taste
1-1/2 cups salad oil

Whisk egg yolk until creamy. Add remaining ingredients, except the oil, and blend well. Slowly drizzle in the oil, whisking constantly, until oil is incorporated and dressing is creamy. This may also be done in a blender. The secret is to add the oil slowly so it incorporates completely. Chill.

Macadamia Nut-Crusted Ono:

4 ono (wahoo) fillets,
   6 ounces each
1/8 cup light olive oil
1 teaspoon fresh ginger, minced
1 teaspoon fresh garlic, minced
salt and pepper to taste
1/4 cup panko (Japanese-style
   crispy bread crumbs)
1/4 cup butter, at room
   temperature
1/4 cup macadamia nuts, chopped
1/2 teaspoon fresh basil, minced
1/2 teaspoon fresh dill, minced
1/2 teaspoon fresh thyme,
   minced
1/2 teaspoon paprika

Marinate the ono for 1 hour in the olive oil, ginger, garlic, salt, and pepper. Preheat oven to 375°. Combine panko, butter, macadamia nuts, herbs, and paprika; blend well. Press marinated fish into panko mixture, and bake for 8 to 10 minutes.

Watercolor painting done by artist
Candice Lee, Kamuela, Big Island; fabric by
Hina Lei Creations, Kamuela, Big Island.

Ginger Clam Miso Soup

Serves 4

Dashi, a clear, light broth, provides classic Japanese flavor to soups, dipping sauces, and simmered dishes. Instant stock is available in granules and tea-bag-like bags in the Oriental section of your grocery store, or in Oriental markets. Prepare the instant dashi according to package directions. Regular-strength chicken broth (skimmed of fat) is an acceptable substitute for dashi, though its flavor isn't as subtle.

Don't boil the miso too long or it will have a grainy texture. That's the trick to a good miso. Once the soup comes to a boil, turn it off immediately. It's worth being a little careful.

3 slices fresh ginger
3 cups chicken stock
2 cups water
1/4 cup dried wakame
   (Japanese seaweed)

1-1/2 pounds fresh Manila clams
1/2 teaspoon dashi (dehydrated
   Japanese bonito seasoning granules)
1/4 cup white miso paste

Place ginger with liquids (chicken stock and water) in a pot, and simmer for 15 minutes. Add wakame, clams, dashi, and simmer until clams open. Ladle 1/2 cup of liquid to mix with the miso paste to dilute it. Add diluted miso paste to the soup. Bring to a simmer, and turn off heat. Ladle into small bowls, and garnish with green onions.

Remove ginger slices before serving.

Garnish:

green onions

Hot and Sour Opah Soup

Serves 4

A tongue-tickling soup from Szechwan, China, this Hot and Sour Opah Soup should be served by ladling it into individual Chinese soup bowls, and sprinkling each serving with chopped green onion.

1 opah fillet, about 8 ounces	3 tablespoons cornstarch
1 tablespoon dry sherry	1-1/2 cups Chinese cabbage,
4-1/2 cups chicken broth	thinly sliced
1 can straw mushrooms, liquid	1/4 pound sugar snap peas, ends
removed	snapped and halved diagonally
1 tablespoon Aloha shoyu	1 teaspoon sesame oil
1/4 cup rice vinegar	salt and pepper to taste
1 Hawaiian chili pepper, chopped	

Opah or moonfish get their name from their large, round profile. Fish that are caught in Hawai'i range from 60 to over 200 pounds. Fishermen say that opah are a wandering species, and are often found in the company of tunas and billfish.

Slice opah fillet diagonally into pieces 1/4-inch thick, and 1-1/2-inches square. Place the fish in a bowl, and toss it with the sherry. Cover the bowl, and refrigerate the fish while preparing the rest of the soup.

In a large saucepan, bring 4 cups of broth to a boil, reduce the heat, add the mushrooms, and simmer the ingredients for 3 minutes. Add the shoyu, vinegar, and chili pepper, and bring the mixture back to a simmer.

Place the cornstarch in a small bowl, blend in the remaining 1/2 cup of broth, and add this slowly to the soup, stirring the ingredients constantly until the mixture thickens.

Add the reserved fish, the cabbage, and the peas to the soup, bring the soup back to a simmer, and cook 1 minute longer. Stir in the sesame oil, and salt and pepper to taste.

Garnish:

2 tablespoons green onion, chopped

Green Papaya Abalone Soup

Serves 6

The Glazed Pork is the crowning touch to this elegant soup. I like to slice the pork very thin, and really mound it on the top. If you can't find fresh abalone in the stores, it's fine to substitute with canned abalone.

3 slices ginger
6 cups chicken broth
6 cups water
1/2 pound fresh scallops
2 cups green papaya, 1-inch cubes

1 can abalone, sliced thin
1 pound mustard cabbage, chopped
salt and pepper to taste
Glazed Pork (see recipe below)

In a soup pot, combine ginger, chicken broth, water, and scallops. Bring to a boil, then simmer for 30 minutes.

Add green papaya, and cook 15 minutes more. Add abalone and mustard cabbage, and simmer for 7 minutes. Add salt and pepper to taste.

Top with Glazed Pork, then garnish with cilantro and green onion.

Glazed Pork:

1/2 pound lean pork, sliced thin
2 tablespoons salad oil
3 tablespoons Aloha shoyu
2 teaspoons sherry wine
1/2 teaspoon granulated sugar
1 tablespoon cornstarch
2 tablespoons water

In a saucepan, sauté the pork. Add shoyu, sherry wine, and sugar, and cook until liquid evaporates. Add mixture of cornstarch and water to create a shiny glazed pork.

Garnish:

6 cilantro sprigs (2 sprigs per serving)
6 tablespoons green onion, chopped
(2 tablespoons per serving)

Canned abalone, although very expensive, is a good substitute for fresh abalone. Marinate and serve as a salad, or use thin slices as a garnish for stir-fries. Heat canned abalone just long enough to heat through; if overcooked, it will toughen.

ECCO DOMANI
ITALIAN WHITE WINE

1996
PINOT GRIGIO
DELLE
VENEZIE
INDICAZIONE GEOGRAFICA TIPICA
IMPORTED BY ECCO DOMANI USA, INC., SANTA ROSA CA, ALC. 12% BY VOL.

Green papaya turtle carving made by Raymond M. Yamasaki, of Ray's Oriental Designs, Kamuela, Big Island; anthuriums donated by Eric S. Tanouye of Green Point Nursery, Hilo, Big Island; antique bowl lent by Jean Nakahara of Antique Sakae, Hilo, Big Island; fabric by Hina Lei Creations, Kamuela, Big Island.

Sam's Shrimp and Papaya Salad

Serves 4

A cool, crunchy shrimp salad on a hot summer afternoon—who could want for more? Place this on a lanai table as the sun is setting, pour a glass of chilled white wine, and enjoy the refreshing flavors.

1 large green papaya, peeled, seeded, and cut in 1/2-inch cubes

2 tomatoes, cut in 1/2-inch cubes

1 tablespoon fresh cilantro, chopped

1 medium cucumber, peeled and cut in 1/2-inch cubes

4 tablespoons macadamia nuts, chopped

2 tablespoons Maui (sweet) onion, diced

2 tablespoons green onion, thinly sliced

1/2 cup macadamia nut oil

2 tablespoons fish sauce

1/2 teaspoon sambal oelek (chili paste)

1 tablespoon rice vinegar

12 large shrimp, peeled and deveined

1 tablespoon macadamia nut oil, for sauté

salt and pepper to taste

1 tablespoon black goma, toasted (black sesame seeds)

Honey Lime Vinaigrette (see recipe below)

In a large bowl, mix the papaya, tomato, cilantro, cucumber, macadamia nuts, Maui onion, green onion, macadamia nut oil, fish sauce, sambal oelek, and vinegar.

Sauté shrimp in 1 tablespoon macadamia nut oil. Add salt and pepper to taste. When done, toss them with the toasted black goma.

Place the papaya mixture in the center of a plate or a martini glass. Arrange shrimp, and serve Honey Lime Vinaigrette on the side.

Honey Lime Vinaigrette:

1/4 cup honey

1 mango or papaya, puréed

juice from 3 fresh limes

1 teaspoon fresh lime zest

3 tablespoons sesame oil

1/2 cup light olive oil

1 teaspoon wasabi (Japanese horseradish paste)

salt and fresh ground white pepper to taste

Blend together, and set aside.

Green papaya is a popular ingredient in Thai and Laotian dishes. Papaya, native to these lands, are tart and crunchy softball-sized fruit that are picked and eaten green. Green papayas are available in some Oriental markets. If you can't find them, substitute with carrots.

1996

The word Anapamu means 'rising place' in the Native American Chumash language.

ANAPAMU

BARREL FERMENTED

Chardonnay

CENTRAL COAST

13.5% Alcohol by Volume

Martini etched glass and sauce container made by Jennifer Pontz of Tropical Art Glass, Holualoa, Big Island; quilt by Bonnie Miki of Kona Kapa, Inc., Kailua-Kona, Big Island; lei made by Marie McDonald and Roen Hufford, Kamuela, Big Island.

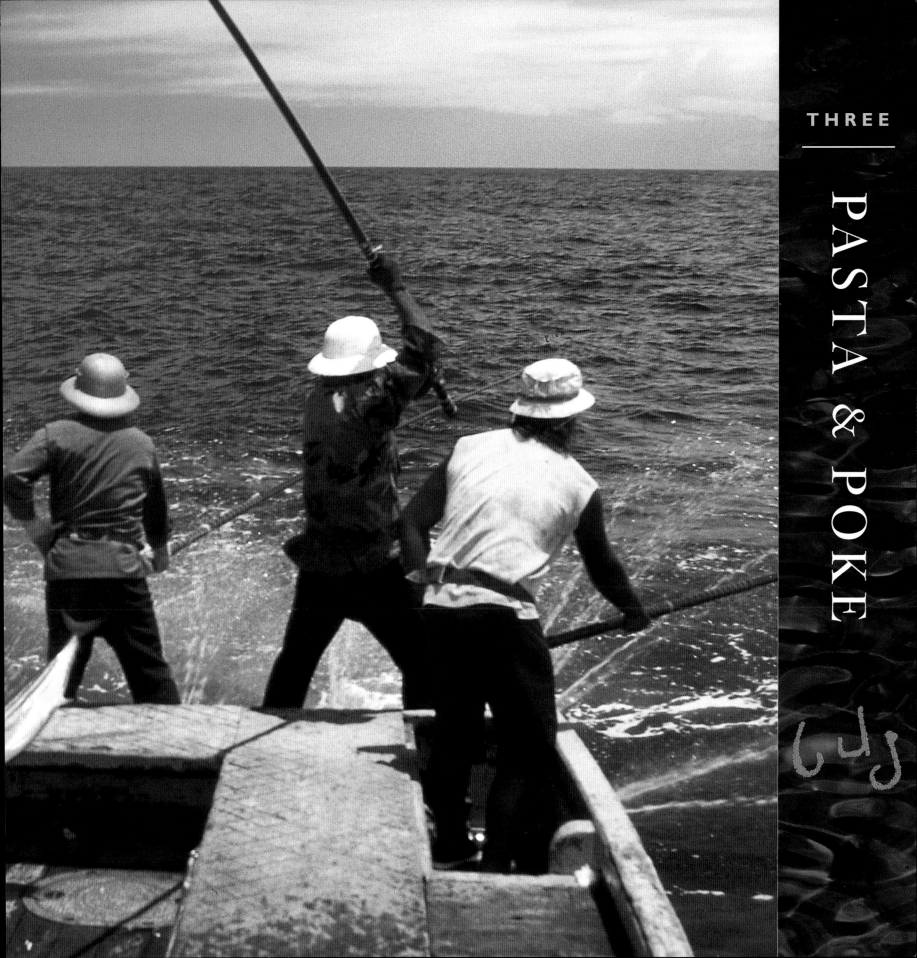

THREE

PASTA & POKE

3

Bottom Fishing

The first time I ever tasted 'opakapaka, I said, "Where did you get this fish?"

"It's a bottom fish," my uncle said. "You have to go out in a boat, and drop a bottom-fishing bag."

And one day I went with my uncles to fish for 'opakapaka.

It's a very unconventional kind of fishing. But for amazing fish, for the most tender white meat—the kind you can get only from deep ocean pools—this is the only way. The water is different down there, you know. You fish at 65 fathoms and more, sometimes to over 100 fathoms, and there really are pools where the deep-water ocean streams eddy around pinnacles, and the fish that live there don't have to swim so fast. They cruise around, and they're way more tender than the fast tuna and marlin above.

The translations of their names tell you: kalekale means soft or spongy, and the kalekale is the fourth (and final) stage of growth of the 'opakapaka, the blue snapper, a highly prized bottom fish; or the hapu'upu'u, the grouper or sea bass, with meat like the most favored taro, which is also called hapu'upu'u; the 'ula'ula or red snapper, which again has a similarly named taro, 'ula'ula (red-red), and is known in the Islands more commonly by its Japanese name: onaga.

But these are the kinds of fish famous for their white-to-pinkish meat and delicate taste, almost as sweet as lobster. You have to find the right pinnacle, the right hole. Experienced fishermen know where to go. They sail way out, and drop a lead-weighted canvas bag filled with chum and baited hooks. We call it the "make dog," that's make in Hawaiian, meaning dead, dead dog. When the bag reaches the desired depth, a string is pulled and the lead weights unravel the bag, spreading the chum. The fish start swarming for the chum, and they hit the hooks.

In the old days we had to hand-line the fish, but now fishermen use hydraulic pullers, and the fish come up much easier.

Bottom fishing is sometimes called "still fishing," because you don't troll. It's vertical fishing, straight down and straight up. As unusual as this kind of fishing is, it yields unusually fine fish, some of the most popular on Island tables.

Kona Fisherman's Wife's Pasta

Serves 4

The scallops in this dish give the pasta a bright flavor the whole family (and your guests) will love. Be sure to let the mixture sit for a few minutes so the scallop juice and aroma can influence the rest of the ingredients. This is a recipe that seems quite simple, but its flavor is unforgettable.

1 pound bow-tie pasta
1/4 cup light olive oil
1 pound bay scallops
1 tablespoon fresh garlic, chopped
1/2 cup carrots, shredded

1/2 cup cabbage, kale, or Swiss chard, shredded
1/4 cup red pepper, julienned
1/4 cup yellow pepper, julienned
salt and pepper to taste

Just a little over 400 species of scallops are sold in the United States. The smallest are calico scallops harvested from the Carolinas to the Gulf of Mexico. Sometimes passed off as the more expensive bay scallops, the calicos are much cheaper, and a little smaller.

Cook pasta according to directions on package, and set aside.

Heat oil in a wok. Stir-fry scallops at medium-high temperature for about 30 seconds. Add garlic, and cook for 30 seconds more. Toss in vegetables, and stir-fry for 30 seconds more. Season with salt and pepper. Then add pasta to the mix, and cook for another minute.

Pour into a pasta bowl, sprinkle with Parmesan cheese and chopped parsley, and ENJOY!

Garnish:

1/2 cup Parmesan cheese, freshly grated
parsley, chopped

Chinese Pasta
with Sesame-Crusted Opah

Serves 4

This recipe combines the rich taste of perfectly cooked opah with a light, and fresh bed of flash-cooked vegetables and pasta. The culinary balance will satisfy every palate. Sit back, and wait for the compliments from your dinner guests.

Opah don't travel in schools. Individual fish are harvested by long-line fleets anchored over seamounts where the opah congregate. Opah have no set migratory pattern, but fishermen believe that they move vertically up the steep slopes of seamounts in search of food. In Island waters there is a good year-round supply of opah with peak quantities caught during the months between April and August.

1 pound linguine or your favorite pasta
1 tablespoon light olive oil
1 tablespoon butter
1 clove fresh garlic, minced
1 medium red bell pepper, cut in strips
1 carrot, cut into thin strips
2 medium zucchinis, trimmed but not peeled, sliced
1/2 pound fresh broccoli florets
1/2 pound fresh asparagus, cut in 1-inch pieces
1/2 pound whole sugar snap peas
6 green onions, sliced thin
2 tablespoons fresh Thai basil
1/4 cup fresh cilantro, chopped
1 tablespoon Aloha shoyu
salt and pepper to taste
1/4 cup Parmesan cheese
Sesame-Crusted Opah (see recipe below)

Cook pasta according to directions on the package.

Meanwhile, heat the oil and butter in a wok. Add the garlic, then all the vegetables, toss and cook 1 to 2 minutes. Add basil, cilantro, shoyu, salt, and pepper. Cook 1 minute more. Add linguine and Parmesan cheese to vegetable mixture, and toss. Serve on warm platter. Top with Sesame-Crusted Opah.

Sesame-Crusted Opah:
4 opah fillets, 6 ounces each
1 large egg, beaten
1/4 cup black goma (black sesame seeds)
1/4 cup white sesame seeds
1/4 cup salad oil
salt and pepper to taste

Season fish with salt and pepper. Mix black goma and white sesame seeds. Dip fish into beaten eggs, then coat with sesame seeds. Heat oil in skillet, and sauté fish for 2 to 3 minutes on each side until golden brown.

Ceramic plate by Ronald Y. Hanatani of RYH Pottery, Volcano, Big Island; ceramic vase and tiles by Kyle Ino of Kyle Ino Designs, Kane'ohe, O'ahu; flowers donated by Marie McDonald and Roen Hufford, Kamuela, Big Island.

Color Coa Poke
with Red Ogo

Serves 6

Color coa, sometimes spelled kalakoa (means all different colors). I've created a colorful, spicy poke combo dish that gets its kick from the 'inamona, a relish of mashed kukui nut. The word "'inamona" is probably a contraction of 'ina'i momona, meaning sweet garnish. Enjoy this surprising and mouth-watering concoction.

1 cup 'ahi, about 1/2 pound, diced
1 cup ono, about 1/2 pound, diced
1 cup calamari, about 1/2 pound, cooked
1/4 cup green onion, chopped
1/4 cup round onion, diced

2 tablespoons sesame oil
2 tablespoons sesame seeds
2 tablespoons Aloha shoyu
1 teaspoon 'inomona (roasted, ground, and salted kukui nut meat)
1/4 cup red or green ogo, chopped

Mix ingredients together. Serve chilled.

In old Hawai'i, ono was broiled, salted, dried, or baked in the imu. It was also eaten raw. The old Hawaiians said that the ono was the "parent" of the 'opelu. They meant that the ono was a blood relative to the 'opelu or that the ono accompanied the 'opelu as a protector.

Tofu Poke
with Red Ogo

Serves 4

I serve this poke in my restaurants on the vegetarian menu. You deep-fry the tofu, and toss it all together with the shoyu and ogo. Amazing! It's great for times when you feel like having a meat-free day. You get your protein, iron, Vitamin C. It's a healthful meal.

3 beefsteak tomatoes, diced
1 pound firm tofu, cubed, dusted with cornstarch, and deep-fried
1 Maui (sweet) onion, diced
1/4 cup green onion, diced
pinch of Hawaiian salt
1 teaspoon dried pepper flakes

2 tablespoons Aloha shoyu
1 tablespoon sesame oil
1 tablespoon black goma (black sesame seeds)
1 tablespoon 'inomona (roasted, ground and salted kukui nut meat)
1/4 cup red ogo, chopped

Lomi (massage) all ingredients together, and ENJOY!

Tofu is a high-protein food made from soybeans—soaked, cooked, and puréed, then coagulated into curd with Epsom salts and vinegar. The custardy cakes, packed in water, then in plastic tubs, come in soft, medium-firm, and firm consistencies. Though quite bland on its own, tofu readily absorbs the flavors of other foods, making it a useful extender.

Marinated Poke
in Coconut Milk

Serves 4

Although "poke" sounds exotic, people have been eating these raw fish dishes for centuries. In Latin countries they call it "seviche," or pickled fish. They are spicy dishes that allow the fish meat to "cook" in lime juice.

2 cups fresh shredded coconut
8-ounce fresh 'ahi fillet, diced
1 medium cucumber, diced
   into 1/4-inch pieces
1 medium fresh tomato, diced
   into 1/4-inch pieces
1 round onion, diced
   into 1/4-inch pieces

1/4 cup green onion, chopped
1 tablespoon fresh cilantro,
   chopped
pinch of chili flakes
juice from 1 fresh lime
salt and pepper to taste

Place the fresh shredded coconut in a bowl, and pour 1 cup warm water over it. Let it sit while you're preparing the other ingredients.

Dice the 'ahi, cucumber, tomato, and onion, and place in a mixing bowl. Chop the green onion and cilantro, then add to the other ingredients. Add a pinch of chili flakes. Squeeze the lime juice into the bowl. Gently stir all of the ingredients together. Pour all of the coconut, and its liquid, into a cheesecloth. Squeeze the cheesecloth tight, holding it over the bowl with the poke ingredients, so that the liquid streams onto the poke. Gently toss to coat the 'ahi with the coconut water. Adjust seasoning with salt and pepper.

Place on serving plate, and garnish with cilantro and lime slices.

Garnish:

cilantro
1 fresh lime, cut in slices

Calm currents and warm temperatures during the months of May through September bring large schools of 'ahi to the waters off the Kona coast. The 'ahi swim close to the surface within 800 nautical miles of Hawai'i. Fishermen in longboats, trollers, and gamefishing craft harvest this prized catch year round using handlines with hooks set in deep waters. Yellowfin are found from the ocean surface to depths below 100 fathoms.

Indigo Hills
1995
North Coast
SAUVIGNON BLANC
ALC. 12% BY VOL.

Spicy Poke

Serves 4-6

Oh, yeah! With this poke, you've got to have an icy drink, two-scoops rice, or a cool bowl of fresh poi. Depends on how much chili pepper you use. You can make it "burn da mouth" hot, or just "sweat a little bit." The limu is crunchy, the 'ahi is firm, and the rest is just right.

1 pound fresh 'ahi, 1/2-inch pieces
1 medium tomato, diced
  1/4-inch pieces
1 cup limu, chopped
1/2 cup round onion, chopped
1 cup cucumber, diced
  1/4-inch pieces

1/2 cup green onion, diced
  1/4-inch pieces
2 tablespoons Aloha shoyu
1 teaspoon sesame oil
1/2 teaspoon Hawaiian chili pepper,
  crushed, seeded, and minced
1 teaspoon Kim Chee base
salt and pepper to taste

In a mixing bowl, combine all of the ingredients. Toss gently. Be sure to keep the fish very cold. Add salt and pepper to taste.

Seasonal changes are noticeable in mature Hawaiian 'ahi. The meat caught near the ocean surface in the summer is often soft and watery, and lacks the typical bright red color. This shallow color is called "burnt" tuna. Fishermen say it's caused by spawning, handling techniques, or overheating during capture. There are considerable differences between normal and "burnt" 'ahi in terms of fat content and nutritional value. My restaurants don't use "burnt" 'ahi because of appearance and texture.

GOSSAMER BAY
VINEYARDS
CALIFORNIA
WHITE ZINFANDEL
1995

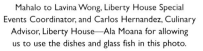

Mahalo to Lavina Wong, Liberty House Special Events Coordinator, and Carlos Hernandez, Culinary Advisor, Liberty House—Ala Moana for allowing us to use the dishes and glass fish in this photo.

Shrimp Scampi
with Green Linguini

Serves 4

Pasta should always be cooked in a large pot filled with boiling salt water. (About 1 gallon of water to 1 pound of pasta.) Keep the water at a rolling boil while the pasta is cooking. After cooking 6 minutes, test for tenderness. Drain at once. Rinse the pasta with either hot or cold water, then with hot water again. If you're serving the pasta on individual plates, toss it with a spoonful or two of oil so it doesn't stick together, then add the sauce.

In this recipe, color makes the stomach grow fonder. The blazing pink-red of the shrimp on the green pasta gives even a connoisseur's eye a really irresistable picture. When I put this dish down before anyone, they always sit back and take in, with real astonishment, what they see. Then they pick up their forks and savor the incredible taste that matches the beauty before them.

1 pound green linguini
1/2 cup butter
1 medium round onion, diced
1 tablespoon fresh garlic, minced
24 fresh shrimp (16-20 pieces per pound), cleaned and deveined

2 teaspoons fresh lemon juice
1 teaspoon Worcestershire sauce
1/4 cup dry white wine
salt and pepper to taste
4 tablespoons fresh cilantro, chopped

Garnish:

1/3 cup Parmesan cheese, freshly grated

Cook pasta according to directions on the package, place on a platter, and keep warm.

Melt butter in a large skillet. Sauté onions and garlic for 30 seconds at medium-high heat. Add shrimp, lemon juice, Worcestershire sauce, and wine, and cook for 1 minute on high heat, stirring constantly. Season with salt and pepper. Add cilantro, and remove from heat.

Pour over warm linguini noodles, and sprinkle with grated Parmesan cheese, and serve immediately.

Spaghetti
with Seafood Tomato Sauce

Serves 4

Traditional spaghetti is made with beef and/or sausage in a tomato-base sauce. My Seafood Tomato Sauce may change your life forever. Imagine this: The sweet flavors of ono, clams, and scallops awash in the spicy zest of tomatoes, peppers, onions, garlic, and white wine. It's the bestest…

About 80 percent of Hawai'i's commercial ono catch is landed by trollers during the months of May through October. The remaining 20 percent is caught in the open ocean by longline fishermen. Ono rarely school, but clusters are sometimes found around buoys, and along banks, pinnacles, and large clumps of flotsam.

1 pound package uncooked spaghetti
1/4 cup light olive oil
1 tablespoon fresh garlic, minced
1 medium round onion, diced
1 bell pepper, diced
1 teaspoon dried oregano
1 teaspoon paprika
1 teaspoon chili flakes
4 tablespoons brown sugar
1/4 cup white wine
1 can (14.5 ounces) diced tomato

1 cup chicken broth
2 tablespoons tomato paste
2 tablespoons cornstarch mixed with
　2 tablespoons water, for thickening
8 ounces scallops, 1-inch diameter
　pieces
1 can (6.5 ounces) minced
　clams, undrained
8 ounces ono, 1-inch chunks
salt and pepper to taste
1/4 cup fresh basil, julienned

Cook spaghetti as directed on the package; drain.

Heat olive oil in wok. Add garlic, onion, and bell pepper. Sauté for 1-1/2 to 2 minutes. Add oregano, paprika, chili flakes, and brown sugar, sauté for 30 seconds. Add white wine, and reduce to half. Add diced tomatoes (with juice), chicken broth, and tomato paste. Simmer for 20 minutes. Thicken with cornstarch mixture.

In separate pan, sauté scallops, clams, and ono with 1 tablespoon olive oil for 1 minute. Add salt and pepper to taste.

Fold in cooked seafood and julienned basil. Pour seafood mixture over spaghetti noodles, and garnish with Parmesan cheese and chopped parsley.

Garnish:

1/2 cup fresh Parmesan cheese, grated
parsley, chopped

Tropical Island Poke

Serves 4-6

An 'ahi's size makes a big difference in the quality and texture of the meat. Small 'ahi have pinkish meat, while larger 'ahi have a deeper red color. The larger the fish, the higher the fat content, a desirable attribute for raw fish and broiling recipes.

I like coming up with interesting flavor combinations that REALLY work. The coconut milk and mango dramatically put the "tropical" in this Island poke. It's an interesting combination of textures—'ahi, mango cubes—soaked in shoyu, sesame oil, and coconut milk. It's a real blend of the South Pacific, Eastern Pacific, and, of course, Hawai'i.

1 pound fresh 'ahi fillet, cut into
  1/2-inch cubes
2 teaspoons sesame oil
3 tablespoons Aloha shoyu
1 teaspoon fresh garlic, finely
  chopped
2 fresh Hawaiian chili peppers,
  finely chopped

1/2 cup coconut milk
1 cup mango, 1/2-inch cubes
1/2 cup red bell pepper,
  1/2-inch cubes
1/4 cup cilantro, chopped
2 tablespoons lemon juice
salt to taste

Combine all ingredients in a bowl, except 'ahi. Mix well. Add 'ahi to mixture, and marinate at least 1 hour before serving. Garnish with chopped cilantro.

Garnish:

cilantro, chopped

Hand-made paper by Lisa Adams of
Spiral Triangle Studios, Volcano, Big Island;
bowl by artist Renee Fukumoto-Ben, Kailua-Kona,
Big Island; lei provided by Tom Pico of Gallerie of
Great Things, Volcano, Big Island.

Smoked Aʻu Poke

Serves 4

There are four species of marlin that are common in tropical and temperate waters: blue marlin and white marlin are found in the Atlantic, striped marlin and black marlin are found in the Pacific. Although marlin and swordfish seem to be kin since they taste alike and both have spearlike bills, they are in different families.

I have friends who go out fishing for marlin to get meat to smoke. It's not completely true, they love the sport and the fight, but I think they love the smoked marlin meat just as much. You can pick up smoked marlin (or aʻu) in shrinkwrapped packages at most local grocery stores.

1 pound smoked aʻu (marlin or swordfish)
1 tablespoon Salt Mixture (see recipe below)
1 teaspoon dried pepper flakes

1-1/2 Maui (sweet) onions, chopped
1/4 cup green onion, chopped
3 beefsteak tomatoes, diced
1 pound firm tofu, cubed, dusted with cornstarch, and deep-fried

Combine ingredients, and store in an air-tight container at room temperature.

Salt Mixture:

1 tablespoon Hawaiian salt
1 tablespoon raw brown sugar
1/8 tablespoon coarse-ground black pepper
1/8 teaspoon garlic powder

Combine and set aside.

Tomato Poke
with Green Ogo and Dry ʻOpae

Serves 4

3 beefsteak tomatoes, diced
1 package dry ʻopae, about 4 ounces
1 Maui (sweet) onion, diced
1/4 cup green onions, diced
pinch of Hawaiian salt
1 teaspoon dry chili flakes
2 tablespoons Aloha shoyu

1 tablespoon sesame oil
1 tablespoon black goma (black sesame seeds)
1 tablespoon ʻinomona (roasted, ground, and salted kukui nut meat)
1/4 cup green ogo, chopped

Lomi (massage) all ingredients together with clean hands, and enjoy.

"Ogo," You Go, I Go Oysters (Yummy)

Serves 6

This is one great pupu. You can serve this as a low-fat pupu. There is no oil. Absolutely none added. Of course, there's oil in the chili pepper and in the sesame seeds if you want to count that. Oh, yeah. There's oil in the oysters. Come on. That's minor, yeah?

24 shucked oysters
1 cup granulated sugar
1 cup Aloha shoyu
1 Hawaiian chili pepper, minced
1 tablespoon fresh ginger, minced
3/4 cup rice vinegar

1/2 Maui (sweet) onion, very
  thinly sliced
2 tablespoons green onion, minced
2 tablespoons sesame seeds
1 pound ogo, chopped

Most of the oysters sold here in Hawai'i are Pacific oysters from the West Coast. Almost all Pacific oysters are harvested from farms rather than in the wild. They were brought to the United States from Japan in the early 1900s in an effort to revitalize the West Coast oyster industry. The only true, native West Coast oyster is the small Olympia, regarded as a delicacy.

Shuck and clean oysters, and lay out on a serving platter. In a large mixing bowl, add sugar, shoyu, chili peppers, ginger, vinegar, and mix well. Mix until sugar is dissolved. Add the onion, green onions, sesame seeds, and ogo. Scoop small amounts onto oysters, sit back, and ENJOY! Yummy!!!

Lobster Poke

Serves 4

This poke has a very refined flavor. Raw lobster is naturally sweet. The crunchy combination of cucumbers, peppers, and ogo, mixed with the sesame oil, chili peppers, and 'inamona, blend into a cool, hot, sweet, spicy taste. It is one good poke.

2 whole fresh raw lobster tails,
  Maine or Spiny, cut into sections
2-1/2 tablespoons ogo
1 tablespoon 'inamona (roasted,
  ground and salted kukui nut meat)
  or macadamia nut oil

Hawaiian salt to taste
1/2 teaspoon sesame oil
1 or 2 Hawaiian chili peppers (depending upon how hot you want it)
1/2 cup cucumber, diced
1/2 cup red bell pepper, diced

Lobster lovers insist that females have more meat. To determine the sex of a lobster, look at its underbelly. There are two small swimmerets at the point where the tail meets the body. If the swimmerets are soft and feathery, it's a female; if they're hard, it's a male.

Cut lobster in pieces, and place in a large mixing bowl. Add all ingredients, and mix well. Serve on a bed of lettuce.

Poke Crabs Medley

Serves 4

The 'a'ama is a large, black, edible crab that runs over shore rocks. The literal meaning for this Hawaiian word is "swift, strong warrior." Other crab facts: Soft shell crabs must be caught just as they have shed their hard shells. The shell starts to toughen within hours, leaving fishermen little time to catch the sea creatures.

This was a winner in the inaugural Sam Choy's Aloha Festival Poke Recipe Contest held in Waimea Park in 1992. It was published in *West Hawai'i Today* on July 8, 1997 in a column by Genny Wright-Hailey (a judge at the contest that year). The grand prize winner was Karen L.U. Won of Kane'ohe, O'ahu.

1 Kona crab
2 white crabs
2 'a'ama crabs
2 tablespoons 'inamona (roasted, ground and salted kukui nut meat)

1 tablespoon 'alaea salt (red Hawaiian salt)
1 teaspoon chili pepper flakes

Remove back shells and gills from crabs; do not remove claws or legs. Wash and drain crabs; let drain in the refrigerator.

Rinse ogo; chill.

Chop Kona crab into eight pieces; white crabs into 4 pieces each; a'ama crabs into 2 pieces each.

Combine 'inamona, salt, and chili pepper flakes; sprinkle on crabs.

Serve over green ogo. Garnish with sprigs of red ogo.

Garnish:

red and green ogo (seaweed)

Kona Cuisine Ulua Poke
with Oriental Citrus Vinaigrette

Serves 4

Here's a very tasty, refreshing salad that has a nice crunchy texture to it. Very outstanding. Be sure to serve immediately after you prepare it. Freshness is a key to its success.

12-ounce fresh ulua fillet, thinly sliced into strips
1 tablespoon ginger, pickled
1 tablespoon fresh ginger, julienned

1 tablespoon langkyo (Japanese pickled onion), julienned
1 cup wonton strips, deep-fried
1/2 cup Citrus Vinaigrette (see recipe below)

In a bowl, toss ulua strips, pickled ginger, fresh ginger, langkyo, and wonton strips.

Place iceberg lettuce on a platter, and top with the ulua poke. Garnish with cilantro, green onion, and macadamia nuts. Serve chilled with Citrus Vinaigrette.

Citrus Vinaigrette:

1 cup balsamic vinegar
1 cup fresh orange juice
salt and pepper to taste
2 tablespoons fresh basil, chopped
2 tablespoons fresh cilantro, chopped
2 tablespoons granulated sugar
1 teaspoon dry mustard
1 pint light olive oil

Garnish:

2-1/2 cups iceberg lettuce, shredded
1/4 cup fresh cilantro, chopped
1/4 cup green onion, chopped
2 tablespoons macadamia nuts, chopped

Combine all ingredients, except oil. Whisk until sugar is completely dissolved and mixture is thoroughly blended. Gradually add oil while continuing to whisk. Readjust seasoning with salt, pepper, and sugar. It is important to dissolve all the sugar before getting the true taste. Keep whisking until mixed well. Makes approximately 2 quarts.

In old Hawai'i, ulua, or crevally jack, were eaten either raw or cooked. Larger ulua were usually baked, and the smaller ones broiled. There are two very general classifications for Hawaiian ulua—they are either dark or light. Within these groupings are many different color combinations and sizes, with unique snout designs.

GOSSAMER BAY
VINEYARDS
CALIFORNIA
SAUVIGNON BLANC
1995

ALC. 11.5% BY VOL. 632201F

Lu'au Shrimp Pasta

Serves 4

Here's a surprisingly easy, and very quick gourmet meal that will astonish your guests. The trick is in the ingredients, which you can get in any supermarket. The shrimp you'll find in the meat or frozen foods section. If you can't locate lu'au leaves (and these are more and more common in good supermarkets), there's always spinach, which tastes almost the same and certainly has the identical nutritive value. Remember, the presentation features bright green and vibrant pink. Color makes the stomach happy.

3 tablespoons butter
1 medium onion, diced
1 tablespoon fresh garlic, minced
2 cups chicken broth
1 cup cooked lu'au leaves, chopped
1/2 cup coconut milk

1 tablespoon fresh Parmesan cheese, freshly grated
24 medium shrimp
8 ounces penne pasta, cooked

TURNING LEAF.
CALIFORNIA
Chardonnay
1996

Heat butter in saucepan. Sauté onions and garlic until onions are translucent. Add chicken broth and lu'au leaves, and cook for about 10 minutes. Then add coconut milk and cheese, and cook for 5 minutes. And finally, add shrimp and cook for about 2 minutes.

Toss lu'au/shrimp mixture with cooked pasta. Cook about 1 minute more, just enough to heat pasta through.

Pour into bowl, sprinkle with cheese, and garnish with diced tomatoes.

Garnish:

Parmesan cheese
tomatoes, diced

64s

Coconut placemat from Peggy Chesnut of Chesnut and Company, Holualoa, Big Island; fabric by Hina Lei Creations, Kamuela, Big Island; ceramic plate by R. Jeff Lee of Lee Ceramics, Waialua, O'ahu; flowers donated by Eric S. Tanouye of Green Point Nursery, Hilo, Big Island.

FOUR

FISH

Net Fishing

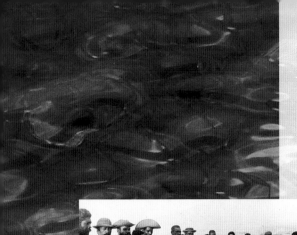

BISHOP MUSEUM

The North Shore and Windward Oʻahu, where I grew up—ho, there are plenty of spots all over where you can go out with a net and pull in amazing catches, the most ʻono (delicious) fish ever.

Usually net fishing is done with partners. The hukilau involves dozens of people and a seine net more than a hundred yards long. "Huki" means pull, and "lau" means leaf, because of the long ti leaves tied to the net to look like seaweed. The belly of the net swells out when it fills with fish. Nothing bonds neighbors better than an activity like this, catching and sharing the sea's bounty.

My high school buddies and I used to go paʻipaʻi net fishing, outside Haleʻiwa at night. Paʻipaʻi means "slap" in Hawaiian. We'd wade out where the fish liked to school. Some of us held the net and others slapped the water—paʻipaʻi—to drive the fish in. The net moved and shifted when the fish hit. Then we'd take the net ashore, pull out the fish and put them in coolers, rinse and straighten the mesh, and go out again.

Solo net fishing involves a throw net, a circle of finely braided meshes with lead weights around the outside. Watching a good throw-net fisherman is like watching a dancer or athlete. There's such grace in the movements. My father-in-law, Mr. Green, one of the best throw-net fishermen on Windward Oʻahu, taught me the art. I could never throw like he did with his decades of practice, but I got pretty good. The trick was to wait for white water so the fish couldn't see the shadow of the net.

The best thing about the net fishing we did was it never damaged the fish—no hook, no spear. So the small fish and fish we didn't want, we put back and they were fine. Leaving nets out overnight or for too long a time (there are laws in Hawaiʻi against this) drowns the fish. My friends, family, and I always took home only what we could eat, and I still practice this rule no matter what kind of fishing I do.

Macadamia Nut Mahimahi
with Chili-Papaya-Pineapple Chutney

Serves 4

Hawai'i has been touted as a "melting pot" where all cultures come together. Just as a small example of how that works, this recipe includes: mahimahi, a fish caught primarily in Hawaiian waters; panko, a Japanese-style breading; and an Indian-style spicy, sweet chutney.

1/2 cup macadamia nuts, chopped
1-1/2 cup panko (Japanese-style crispy bread crumbs)
8 mahimahi fillets, 3 ounces each
salt and white pepper to taste
1 cup all-purpose flour

2 eggs, beaten
1/4 cup vegetable oil, for frying (more oil may be needed)
Chili-Papaya-Pineapple Chutney (see recipe below)

When mahimahi started being used in fine restaurants, someone made the mistake of mentioning that it was a dolphinfish. People got so upset, thinking they were eating "Flipper," that they shied away from the fish. Just to get the record straight, mahimahi is a fish and, therefore, not even a close relative to the dolphin, which is a mammal.

Mix macadamia nuts and panko for breading.

Season mahimahi fillets with salt and white pepper. Dredge in flour, dip in eggs, then dredge in panko/macadamia nut breading.

Heat oil in a skillet, add breaded mahimahi, and cook for 2 minutes on each side.

Serve with Chili-Papaya-Pineapple Chutney.

Chili-Papaya-Pineapple Chutney:

1 small fresh pineapple, peeled, cored, and chopped
1 medium fresh papaya, seeded, peeled, and chopped
1 tablespoon fresh ginger, minced
6 tablespoons granulated sugar
1 tablespoon sambal oelek (chili paste)

In a medium saucepan, combine all ingredients, except chili paste. Cook on medium heat 1 hour or until mixture has a syrupy consistency. Fold in sambal oelek (chili paste).

Steamed Onaga
with Pickled Ginger and Scallions

Serves 2

Steamed fish doesn't lose its flavor like other meats. And in this recipe, I've paid close attention to preserve the delicate taste of good, fresh onaga. The ginger, onions, and Shiitake mushrooms add a nice, spicy flavor.

1 fresh whole onaga (red snapper), 2-1/2 pounds, cleaned and scaled
1 cup fresh shiitake mushrooms, sliced
1/2 cup pickled ginger, very thin julienne slices
1/2 cup green onion, thinly sliced diagonally
1/2 cup cilantro, coarsely chopped
3/4 cup peanut oil
1 tablespoon sesame oil
1/4 cup Aloha shoyu
salt and pepper to taste

On a platter, score onaga diagonally in two directions to make diamonds. Season with salt and pepper. Sprinkle sliced shiitake mushrooms around the platter edge. Put platter in the steamer, and cook for 15 minutes, or until done.

Remove fish platter from steamer, and sprinkle fish with pickled ginger and green onion. Set aside.

Heat peanut oil until smoking, then pour over ginger and green onions. Oil should be so hot it sizzles as you pour it. Pour shoyu on fish, then drizzle with sesame oil, and garnish with roasted sesame seeds and cilantro.

Garnish:

roasted sesame seeds
cilantro, coarsely chopped

ECCO DOMANI®
ITALIAN WHITE WINE

— 1996 —
PINOT GRIGIO
DELLE
VENEZIE

INDICAZIONE GEOGRAFICA TIPICA
IMPORTED BY ECCO DOMANI USA, INC, SANTA ROSA CA. ALC. 12% BY VOL.

Blackened Ono

Serves 4

The mild flavor of ono works very well with the spicy, hot blackened coating in this recipe. This type of flavoring is from the deep South, and introduced by Cajun chefs. To add a local flare, I've included a Shoyu Butter Sauce to top off this tasty dish.

8 ono (wahoo) fillets, 4 ounces each
3 tablespoons Blackening Spice
   Mixture (see recipe below)

Shoyu Butter Sauce
   (see recipe below)
3 tablespoons vegetable oil

Ono are generally deep steel-blue with a whitish underbelly. Older fish have brownish or black stripes that run the length of their roundish bodies. They have a camouflage defense that allows them to blend into their environment. Fishermen say, "Watch out for the teeth. They bite anything: lines, nets, fingers…"

Season ono fillets with Blackening Spice Mixture. Heat oil until it smokes. Sear fish for 3 minutes on each side. Serve Shoyu Butter Sauce with fish, and garnish with lemon wedges.

Blackening Spice Mixture:

2 tablespoons paprika
1/2 teaspoon ground cayenne pepper
1 teaspoon black pepper, ground
1 teaspoon dried oregano leaves
1 teaspoon dried thyme leaves
1 teaspoon garlic salt
1 teaspoon onion salt
1/2 teaspoon white pepper

Blend all ingredients, and set aside. Store in refrigerator in an air-tight container.

Shoyu Butter Sauce:

1 tablespoon Aloha shoyu
1 tablespoon brown sugar
6 tablespoons butter, melted
juice of 1/2 lemon
2 tablespoons light olive oil

Blend all ingredients, and set aside.

Garnish:

lemon wedges

GALLO *of* SONOMA
SONOMA COUNTY
Cabernet Sauvignon

Seared Albacore Tuna
with Coconut-Ginger Sauce

Serves 4

Albacore is also known by its Japanese name, tombo 'ahi. The names are sometimes a little confusing. There are so many different kinds of tuna that are known as 'ahi. Once marinated, the albacore tuna steaks are perfect for searing. I added a Coconut-Ginger Sauce for a touch of sweetness.

Albacore tuna is a type of 'ahi. The Hawaiian name that specifically describes the albacore is 'ahipalaha. "Palaha" means flat. So the albacore tuna is a small 'ahi, possibly a fish in a young stage of growth, with a flat body. It's also known as a yellowfin tuna in very general terms.

4 albacore tuna steaks, 6 ounces
   each, and 3/4-inch thick
2 tablespoons oil

Seafood Marinade (see recipe below)
Coconut-Ginger Sauce
   (see recipe below)

Marinate tuna steaks in Seafood Marinade for 10 minutes.

Heat oil in a frying pan over high heat. Sear marinated tuna for 2 minutes on each side. Serve hot with warm Coconut-Ginger Sauce.

Seafood Marinade:

1 cup Aloha shoyu
1 tablespoon oyster sauce
1 tablespoon sesame oil
1/2 cup brown sugar
1 tablespoon cilantro, chopped
1 teaspoon chili flakes
1 teaspoon garlic, minced
1/4 teaspoon Chinese 5-Spice powder

Mix all ingredients until sugar is dissolved.

Coconut-Ginger Sauce:
1 can coconut milk
1/4 cup sugar
1 tablespoon ginger, minced
1-1/2 tablespoons cornstarch mixed
   with 3 tablespoons water for thickening
salt and pepper to taste

In a saucepan, combine coconut milk, sugar, and ginger. Bring to a boil. Mix cornstarch and water together, and whisk into coconut milk and ginger sauce to thicken. Add salt and pepper to taste.

Plate provided by Liberty House—Ala Moana, Honolulu, O'ahu; flowers donated by Amy and Mike Rosato of Island Orchid, Kailua-Kona, Big Island; fabric by Jan of Hina Lei Creations, Kamuela, Big Island; greenery donated by Eric S. Tanouye of Green Point Nursery, Hilo, Big Island.

Weke 'Ula
with Shoyu Ginger Sauce & Roasted Sesame Butter

Serves 2

Weke 'ula are named for their red color once they have been extracted from the water. In fact, fishermen say that while the weke 'ula are swimming in their schools, they look yellow. They just turn red when taken out of the water.

The weke 'ula, one of my dad's favorite fish to deep-fry, is a red surmullet with very large scales. I've added the sesame butter and shoyu ginger sauces to bring out the natural flavor of this fish.

1 weke 'ula, about 2 pounds
 (substitute with trout or salmon,
 or other 2-pound fish)
1/2 cup cornstarch
salt and pepper to taste

3 cups vegetable oil, for deep-frying
Roasted Sesame Butter
 (see recipe below)
Shoyu Ginger Sauce
 (see recipe below)

Bread fish in cornstarch, and season with salt and pepper. Deep-fry until cooked.

Remove from wok. Pour Shoyu Ginger Sauce over entire fish, then drizzle with Roasted Sesame Butter. Garnish with green onions and cilantro.

Garnish:

1 tablespoon green onion,
 chopped
1 tablespoon fresh cilantro,
 chopped

Shoyu Ginger Sauce:

3 tablespoons Aloha shoyu
1 tablespoon fresh ginger,
 peeled and grated

Combine.

Roasted Sesame Butter:

2 tablespoons roasted sesame
 seeds, crushed
1/4 pound butter, softened
salt and pepper to taste

Blend well.

Ginger Pesto Rice
with Macadamia Nut Mahimahi

Serves 4

Oh, yeah! This one is GOOD. I love ginger pesto, so combined it with a macadamia nut-crusted mahimahi (a favorite in my restaurants). And oh, man, it's a crowd pleaser. This dish is easy to make, real fast, too.

1 cup white rice, steamed,
   then cooled slightly
1/2 cup cilantro, minced
1/2 cup green onion, minced
1/4 cup fresh ginger, minced
3/4 cup vegetable oil
4 mahimahi fillets, 3 ounces each

1 cup all-purpose flour
2 eggs, beaten
1 cup panko (Japanese-style
   crispy bread crumbs)
1/2 cup macadamia nuts, mixed
   together with panko
salt and pepper to taste

In old Hawai'i, mahimahi meat was never eaten raw. It was generally cut into slices and broiled over hot coals, or dried, then cooked. Hawaiians ate the mahimahi roe either raw, or dried, then cooked.

Steam rice according to directions on package. Let cool slightly, then mix in cilantro, green onions, and ginger. Meanwhile, season mahimahi with salt and pepper, then dredge in flour, dip in eggs, then dip into panko/macadamia nut breading. Heat oil in a wok, add breaded mahimahi, and cook about 2 minutes on each side. Remove fish from wok, and place atop cooked rice.

Miso Yaki Salmon

Serves 4

Miso, a favorite seasoning in Japan, is made from fermented soybeans mixed with crushed grain. There are two types commonly available in Oriental markets and local grocery stores—white miso, made with rice; and red miso, made with barley. Miso, both red and white, are available in plastic tubes in the refigerated foods section or on shelves of Oriental markets.

The Japanese use the term "yaki" to describe the grilling of food. So, this is a recipe for grilled salmon seasoned with miso. Serve it over hot rice, sprinkled with roasted sesame seeds, and garnished with a wedge of lemon.

4 salmon fillets, 6 ounces each
Miso Marinade (see recipe below)

Marinate salmon fillets in Miso Marinade for 1 hour. Broil in the oven for 8 to 10 minutes.

Serve with hot rice, and garnish with roasted sesame seeds and lemon wedges.

Miso Marinade:

3/4 cup white miso
3 tablespoons fresh ginger, grated
1/4 cup granulated sugar
1/2 cup Mirin (Japanese sweet rice wine)
1/4 cup rice vinegar

Blend, and set aside.

Garnish:

roasted sesame seeds
lemon wedges

Plate provide by Sam Choy; salt and pepper shakers provided by Rick Clark, Kailua-Kona, Big Island; orchids donated by James McCully Orchids Culture, Hakalau, Big Island

Onaga
with Tropical Herb Salsa

Serves 4

I really like building a dish. Layering of the onaga and salsa magically blends the flavors of this dish. To serve this, you can cut the tower into quarters, or give each person their own salsa-covered fillet. Either way, it's 'ono.

12 onaga fillets, 2-1/2 ounces each
1/4 cup all-purpose flour
salt and pepper to taste

1/4 cup vegetable oil
Tropical Herb Salsa
 (see recipe below)

Dust the fish with flour, and season with salt and pepper. Heat the oil, in a skillet. Place the fish in hot oil, and cook about 3 minutes on each side, being careful not to overcook.

LAYERING: (from the bottom up)

1 tablespoon Tropical Herb Salsa
1 piece of onaga
1 tablespoon of salsa
1 piece of onaga
1 tablespoon of salsa
1 piece of onaga
1 tablespoon of salsa

Tropical Herb Salsa:

1 tomato, with the seeds, diced
1 papaya, diced
1 red bell pepper, diced
1/2 cup strawberries, diced
1 medium red onion, diced
1/2 cup pineapple, diced
juice of 1 fresh lemon
1/2 cup light olive oil
1 teaspoon salt and pepper
1 bunch fresh cilantro, chopped
1 tablespoon fresh ginger, minced

Combine all ingredients, and mix well.

One of Hawai'i's most important bottom fish, in terms of total landed weight and value, is the onaga or 'ula'ula. The peak season for catching onaga in Hawaiian waters is during the month of December, although they are successfully harvested in the fall and winter months of October through March.

Fresh 'Ahi Clubhouse Sandwich

Serves 1

This is a GREAT sandwich, perfect for an afternoon barbecue, a tailgate party, a Super Bowl party, or a "pau-hana" get-together. Most of the ingredients you probably have sitting around the kitchen. So, what are you waiting for…

2 'ahi fillets (about 2 ounces each)
    per sandwich, marinated, then
    grilled or sautéed in a wok

Yellowfin and bigeye tuna, both called 'ahi, are completely interchangeable for sashimi and other raw fish preparations. Yellowfin can also be substituted with other tunas and with a'u (swordfish or marlin) for grilling, smoking, or drying.

Combine all marinade ingredients and blend well, to taste. Marinate 'ahi fillets in mixture for 5 minutes, or less, then remove fish, and set aside.

Marinade: (one portion makes about 1 cup)

1/2 cup Aloha shoyu
1/4 cup light salad oil
2 tablespoons Mirin
    (Japanese sweet rice wine)
1/4 teaspoon sesame oil
1/2 tablespoon cilantro, minced
2 tablespoons green onion, thinly sliced
1 tablespoon garlic, minced
1 tablespoon ginger, minced
1/2 teaspoon salt
1/4 teaspoon white pepper
1-1/2 teaspoons ground
    Chinese 5-Spice Powder
1 tablespoon black goma
    (black sesame seeds)
1 pinch dried red pepper flakes or
    1 Hawaiian chili pepper

Sandwich Ingredients:

1 slice of fresh pineapple, peeled
    and skinned
3 slices of sourdough bread, toasted
mayonnaise to spread lightly on
    toasted bread
1 piece of butter leaf or Manoa lettuce
2 slices fresh tomato
2 pieces cooked bacon
2 pieces sliced ripe avocado
1 small bunch radish sprouts

Grill fresh fish and pineapple, or place marinated fish and pineapple in a wok that has been heated with 1/4 teaspoon light vegetable oil. Sear 'ahi to medium rare. Separately sear pineapple on both sides. Toast three slices of bread, apply mayonnaise very lightly on one side of all three slices. Start the layering process.

First layer: One slice of toasted bread, 'ahi, pineapple, radish sprouts

Second layer: One slice of toasted bread, lettuce, tomato, bacon, avocado, and radish sprouts.

Last layer: Third slice of bread, and the second piece of 'ahi. Pierce with toothpicks in quarter sections. Serve with taro or potato chips.

Onaga
with Tropical Sweet and Sour Sauce

Serves 4

Onaga is similar to the 'opakapaka in texture and taste, although some will swear that the onaga is softer and more moist. For this dish, the onaga is baked, lightly seasoned, before you add the vegetables and sauce, leaving the natural juices of the fish undiluted.

A bottom fish, onaga is caught in deep waters (100-180 fathoms). They favor outcroppings along rocky bottoms. Most onaga caught in Hawaiian waters range in size from 1 to 18 pounds.

Sweet and Sour Sauce
  (see recipe below)
1 whole fresh onaga, 1 to 3 pounds
salt and pepper to taste
  1/2 cup water

2 tablespoons butter
1/2 cup red onions, 3/4-inch diced
1/4 cup green pepper, 3/4-inch diced
1/4 cup red pepper, 3/4-inch diced
1/2 cup papaya, 3/4-inch diced
1/2 cup pineapple, 3/4-inch diced

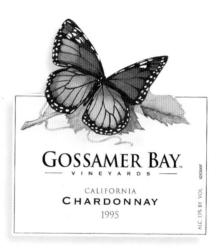

Heat oven to 350°. Prepare Sweet and Sour Sauce, and set aside. Place onaga in a baking pan, season with salt and pepper. Add 1/2 cup water, and cover with foil. Bake at 350° for 25 to 30 minutes. While onaga is baking, melt butter in a saucepan. Sauté onions and peppers for 2 minutes; then add fruit. Cook for 1 minute. Add Sweet and Sour Sauce, and simmer for 4 to 5 minutes. Remove onaga from oven, and place on a fish platter. Pour sauce over the baked onaga. Serve hot.

Sweet and Sour Sauce:

2 tablespoons pineapple juice
1 cup granulated sugar
1/2 cup vinegar
2 teaspoons Aloha shoyu
1/2 cup ketchup
1/2 cup water
1/4 cup orange marmalade
1-1/2 teaspoons ginger, minced
1 teaspoon garlic, minced
1/4 teaspoon hot pepper sauce
1 tablespoon cornstarch blended with
  1/4 cup water for thickening

Bring pineapple juice to a boil. Add sugar, and cook until sugar is dissolved. Add the vinegar, shoyu, ketchup, water, orange marmalade, ginger, garlic, and hot pepper sauce to mixture, and bring to a boil for about 3 to 4 minutes. Make a cornstarch mixture by blending one tablespoon cornstarch with 1/4 cup water. Add cornstarch mixture to sauce, and cook until thickened. Set aside.

Platter by artist Tom Pico, lent by The Gallery of Great Things, Kamuela, Big Island; lauhala mats provided by Auntie Elizabeth Lee of Malu's Enterprise, Kailua-Kona, Big Island.

Sautéed Mahimahi
with Warm Corn Sauce

Serves 4

The warm corn sauce and mashed potatoes in this recipe really give this dish a down-home flavor. The natural sweetness of the corn offsets the mild flavor of the mahimahi.

4 mahimahi fillets, 6 ounces each
1 tablespoon salt
1/2 teaspoon coarse-ground
  black pepper

2 tablespoons light olive oil
Warm Corn Sauce
  (see recipe below)
mashed potatoes

Season the mahimahi with salt and pepper. Warm olive oil in a sauté pan, and cook the mahimahi for 3 to 4 minutes on one side, browning well. Turn the fish, and continue to cook for another 3 minutes.

Place fish on a platter, and serve with Warm Corn Sauce and mashed potatoes.

Warm Corn Sauce:

2 tablespoons butter
1/2 cup round onion, chopped
1 bay leaf
1 clove fresh garlic
1/4 cup dry white wine
2 cups fresh corn kernels
3/4 cup heavy cream
salt and pepper to taste

Place 1 cup of corn kernels in a food processor, and pulverize. Set aside.

Put butter in a saucepan over medium heat. Sauté chopped onions, bay leaf, and garlic. Add white wine, and reduce to half.

Add whole corn kernels and pulverized corn, and sauté. Add heavy cream, then salt and pepper to taste. Simmer sauce for 10 minutes. Remove the bay leaf. Adjust seasonings. Keep warm until ready to serve.

Kuku's Pan-Fried Kalikali

Serves 4

Kuku (Hawaiian for grandparent) is what we called an old woman who lived up the road from our house. When the fishermen came in with kalikali, they always took some to her. When she cooked it, the entire neighborhood smelled like home cooking.

Kalikali, a small red-tail snapper, is harvested in waters just off the shores of the main Hawaiian Islands. Sold at the fish auctions, through intermediary buyers on the major islands, or directly to retail fish markets and restaurants, this Island catch is marketed primarily through the Honolulu fish auction.

4 kalikali (small red-tail snapper) fillets, 6 ounces each (substitute with any other snapper fillets)
1/2 cup all-purpose flour (to dust fish)
1/4 cup vegetable oil
4 tablespoons butter

1 medium round onion, diced
2 cloves garlic, minced
2 cups fresh shiitake mushrooms, sliced
1 cup tomatoes, diced
2 tablespoons Aloha shoyu
salt and pepper to taste

Season fish fillets with salt and pepper, and dust with flour. Heat oil in a frying pan. Pan-fry fish, skin-side down, for 2 to 3 minutes until golden brown, then turn, and fry another 2 or 3 minutes. Remove fish, and keep warm without overcooking.

Heat pan. Add butter. Sauté onions and garlic over medium heat, until translucent. Add fresh mushrooms, and sauté for 2 to 3 minutes. Add diced tomatoes, and sauté for 2 minutes more. Add shoyu, and salt and pepper to taste.

Serve shiitake mushroom sauce over fish, and garnish with green onions.

Garnish:

green onion, chopped

Ginger Pesto-Crusted 'Opakapaka
with Coconut Cream Sauce

Serves 4

If the Coconut Cream Sauce is thin, don't panic. All you need to do is add some cornstarch mixture to the simmering sauce, and cook for another minute. Adjust the seasoning with salt and pepper.

8 fresh 'opakapaka (pink snapper) fillets, 3-ounce pieces
1 tablespoon oil, for frying

Ginger Pesto Sauce (see recipe below)
Coconut Cream Sauce (see recipe below)

Marinade 'opakapaka in cooled Ginger Pesto Sauce for 1 to 2 minutes. Place fillet in a frying pan, and cook for 1-1/2 to 2 minutes on each side over medium-high heat.

Pour 2 ounces of Coconut Cream Sauce on each of 4 serving plates. Arrange two pieces of fish on each plate, and drizzle with Ginger Pesto Sauce.

Ginger Pesto Sauce:

1/2 cup fresh cilantro, minced
1/2 cup green onion, minced
1/4 cup fresh ginger, minced
3/4 cup peanut oil
1 tablespoon Aloha shoyu
salt and white pepper to taste

Place cilantro, green onions, and ginger in a deep bowl. Heat peanut oil in a pan until smoking. Pour heated oil over cilantro, green onions, and ginger. BE CAREFUL: THE OIL WILL BE SIZZLING, AND VERY HOT. Add shoyu, and salt and white pepper to taste.

Coconut Cream Sauce:

3 tablespoons butter
1 medium round onion, minced
1 cup heavy cream
2 cups canned coconut milk (unsweetened)
2 tablespoons cornstarch mixed with 1-1/2 tablespoons water, if needed for thickening
salt and pepper to taste

Place butter in a saucepan. Add onions, and cook until translucent. Add heavy cream. Bring to a boil, reduce heat and simmer for 1 to 2 minutes. Add coconut milk, and cook for another 2 minutes.

Garnish:

tomato wedges
straw mushrooms

Valued by foreigners for its tender white meat, 'opakapaka was one of the most commonly requested selections in Hawai'i's restaurants before World War II. Today, up-scale restaurants serve 'opakapaka during the winter months of October through February, when fishing fleets bring in their largest catches.

Plate by Ronald Y. Hanatani of RYH Pottery, Volcano, Big Island; feather lei lent by Danny Akaka, Hawaiian Historian at the Mauna Lani Hotel, Kohala Coast, Big Island; wooden serving tray lent by Liberty House-Ala Moana, Honolulu, O'ahu; ti leaf lei made by Amy and Mike Rosato, Island Orchid, Kailua-Kona, Big Island; vine-ripened tomatoes by Nakano Farms, Waimea, Big Island.

Crunchy Hale'iwa Mahimahi

Serves 2

Until recently, mahimahi was virtually unknown in the United States outside of Hawai'i and Florida. But now that the general population is used to the Hawaiian name, mahimahi has become one of the most requested fish in our nation's restaurants.

The word "crunchy" in the title is used to describe the vegetables, not the fish. It's the very quickly stir-fried onions, carrots, snap peas, and zucchini that give this recipe its name. The fish is unreal 'ono. Eat in good health.

1 tablespoon fresh cilantro, chopped
salt and pepper to taste
1 tablespoon brown sugar
1 tablespoon fresh garlic, minced
1 tablespoon fresh ginger, minced
4 mahimahi fillets, 3 ounces each
2 tablespoons butter

1 Maui (sweet) onion, julienned
1/2 cup carrots, julienned
1/2 cup zucchini, julienned
1-1/2 cups sugar snap peas
1 tablespoon Aloha shoyu
1 tablespoon oyster sauce

Blend cilantro, salt, pepper, brown sugar, garlic, and ginger. Press into the mahimahi fillets to coat, and let stand for about 5 minutes. Meanwhile, heat oil in a heavy skillet. Cook mahimahi fillets for about 2 minutes on each side.

In separate skillet, sauté onions in butter for 30 seconds over medium-high heat. Add carrots, zucchini, and sugar snap peas, and sauté for 2 minutes more. Add shoyu and oyster sauce to hot pan, and cook for 1 minute longer. Remove from heat, and place around the mahimahi.

Deep-Fried Hapuʻupuʻu (Sea Bass)
with Tropical Fruit Salsa

Serves 4

Chinese cuisine traditionally uses sea bass or hapuʻupuʻu for deep-frying
because of its mild flavor. It fries up nice and crisp—tender on the inside,
and crunchy on the outside.

1 whole hapuʻupuʻu (sea bass),
   about 24 inches or 3 to 4 pounds
2-1/2 cups all-purpose flour
salt and pepper to taste

3 cups vegetable oil, for deep-frying
Tropical Fruit Salsa
   (see recipe below)

Mix Tropical Fruit Salsa ingredients together in large mixing bowl. Add marinade.
Toss everything together. Heat oil in wok. Score fish on two sides, and roll in
flour. Deep-fry for 2 to 3 minutes until fish is cooked. Pour Tropical Salsa and
marinade mixture on fish, and serve.

*The hapuʻupuʻu or sea bass is a
good-eating fish with a mild-to-
sweet flavor. It has a large head,
and is reddish-brown or black in
color. There are really two major
types of hapuʻupuʻu found in our
waters, the red and the black.
Both can be caught in the off-shore
reefs of all of Hawaiʻi's major islands.*

Marinade:

1 cup honey
1 tablespoon Aloha shoyu
1 cup fresh orange juice
1/4 cup apple cider vinegar
salt and pepper to taste

Blend, and set aside

Tropical Fruit Salsa:

1/4 cup honeydew melon, diced
1/4 cup cantalope, diced
1/4 cup pineapple, diced
1/4 cup papaya, diced
1/4 cup fresh corn kernels
1/4 cup black beans, cooked and rinsed
1/4 cup white beans, cooked and rinsed
1 tablespoon red onion, chopped
1 tablespoon round onion, chopped

Combine. Serve chilled.

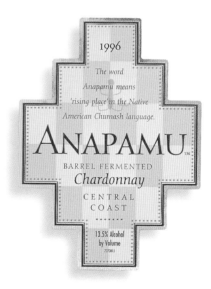

1996

*The word
Anapamu means
'rising place' in the Native
American Chumash language.*

ANAPAMU™

BARREL FERMENTED
Chardonnay

CENTRAL
COAST

13.5% Alcohol
by Volume
2373913

Mahimahi Black Beans
with Stir-Fried Vegetables

Serves 4

I use fermented black beans, a traditional Chinese seasoning, to add an Oriental flair to this dish of mahimahi and stir-fried vegetables. It has a nice, salty taste that blends well with the oyster sauce, shoyu, and the mahimahi.

2 tablespoons salad oil
1 teaspoon ginger, minced
4 cups mixed stir-fried vegetables
1/2 tablespoon oyster sauce
12 pieces mahimahi,
  2 to 3 ounces each
salt and pepper to taste
1/4 cup all-purpose flour
Black Bean Sauce
  (see recipe below)

The mahimahi is a voracious deep sea hunter that loves to feed on 'opelu. They haunt 'opelu feeding grounds. Disappointed 'opelu fishermen usually leave the fishing grounds when a mahimahi comes around. The fishing is spoiled, because the 'opelu are too worried about the mahimahi to eat the bait.

Heat 1 tablespoon salad oil in a wok over high heat. Add 1 teaspoon minced ginger to oil. Stir-fry for about 10 to 15 seconds.

Stir in mixed vegetables, and cook for 2 to 3 minutes, until vegetables are crisp on the outside and tender in the center. Add oyster sauce to mixture. Remove from heat, and set aside.

Season mahimahi with salt and pepper, then dust with flour. Heat skillet and 1 tablespoon oil. Sauté the mahimahi about 1-1/2 minutes on each side. Remove from heat.

Place one piece of mahimahi in the middle of each serving plate. Top with 1/2 cup of mixed stir-fried vegetables. Add another layer of mahimahi, with another 1/2 cup of vegetables. Crown with a final piece of mahimahi. Drizzle with Black Bean Sauce, and garnish with cilantro and ogo.

Garnish:
ogo, cilantro

Black Bean Sauce:
2 tablespoons vegetable oil
2 tablespoons fresh ginger, minced
2 teaspoons fresh garlic, minced
1/2 teaspoon Hawaiian chili pepper, minced, or red chili pepper flakes
2 tablespoons fermented black beans, rinsed and drained
1/4 cup sherry wine
2 tablespoons Aloha shoyu
1 tablespoon oyster sauce

1 tablespoon granulated sugar
1-1/2 cups chicken broth
2 tablespoons cornstarch mixed with 1/4 cup water for thickening

Rinse and drain fermented black beans, and set aside.

In a saucepan, heat oil over medium-high burner. Add ginger, garlic, and chili pepper; then stir-fry for 30 seconds. Add fermented black beans, sherry wine, shoyu, oyster sauce, sugar, and chicken broth. Bring to a boil, reduce heat and simmer for about 15 minutes. Slowly whisk in the cornstarch and water mixture until the sauce thickens. Remove from heat. Keep warm until ready to serve.

Plate provided by Liberty House—Ala Moana, Honolulu, O'ahu; flowers donated by Eric S. Tanouye of Green Point Nursery, Hilo, Big Island.

FIVE

SHELLFISH

Torch Fishing

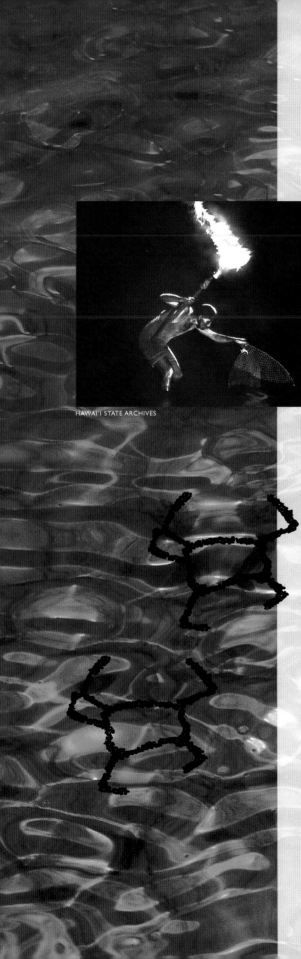

HAWAI'I STATE ARCHIVES

Some of my best memories are of torch fishing with my father in La'ie. I believe that of all the fishing in Hawai'i, torch fishing is the most beautiful. Maybe because it's the most primitive. When you're doing it, you can't help but think of ancient Hawaiians who walked these reefs in the same way, with their torches shining on the dark water.

I would go with my father on calm nights. That's why I say it's the most beautiful. To see those lanterns, deep orange, out there floating above the water, with the reflections in long golden lines, the fishermen standing in their own little worlds, you know, those spheres of lantern light. And it would be my calabash uncles and a few of our neighbors torch fishing.

Nowadays folks use mostly Coleman lanterns, which are bright and very white. Anciently there were real torches, of course, and sometimes pure torch fishermen will still use just basic fire. One night back in the seventies, when our family was driving home from Honolulu, I saw a man out on the reef off Ka'a'awa, and he had a real torch. I'll never forget that sight, like looking back through time at an ancestor.

But growing up we had gas lanterns, and you had to be careful if the wind came up and gusted and you were on the wrong side—you'd get scorched, fry the hair on your arms. Malia nights—calm nights—were best. Moonless. Overcast even better because then it was black-black, not even starlight.

On shore we would start up our lanterns and slip tabbis on our feet to protect from the sharp coral. Mosquitoes came in clouds around the lanterns, but then we'd set off wading, and as we got out farther on the reef, the bugs thinned away. And then—it was like walking into a candy shop, you don't know what candy will catch your eye—we'd look down into the cracks and reef pools and here would be lobsters scuttling up, and crabs, fish that travel only at night, all of this wonderful seafood, the light attracting the goods to you.

Christopher's Crab Cakes
with Herb Sauce

Serves 4

This is a Christopher recipe. He really enjoys crab cakes, and the Herb Sauce is one of his favorites. He doesn't really cook them by himself yet, but he enjoys them so much, it's only a matter of time.

Herb Sauce (see recipe below)
3/4 pound cooked crab meat
1-1/4 cups fresh bread crumbs
1 large whole egg, beaten
3 tablespoons Maui (sweet) onion,
  finely chopped

1 teaspoon salt
1 teaspoon ground mustard
1/4 teaspoon garlic, minced
4 tablespoons butter

Crab cakes are often extremely rich, made with lots of melted butter, whole eggs, or, perhaps, mayonnaise. It's possible to reduce the fat content a little by substituting margarine for butter, and low-fat mayonnaise for the regular mayo. You can use canned or (fresh) lump crab meat, and in extreme cases, you can use imitation meat. I don't recommend it, though.

Prepare Herb Sauce, and set aside.

Mix crab cake ingredients, except lemon wedges. Shape mixture into 6 patties, each about 3 inches in diameter.

Melt butter in pan over medium-high heat. Add crab cakes, and sauté about 3 minutes on each side, until golden brown. Serve with Herb Sauce and lemon wedges.

Herb Sauce:

2 tablespoons fresh dill or
  fresh tarragon leaves, chopped
1 teaspoon fresh chives, chopped
2 teaspoons fresh cilantro, chopped
1 teaspoon fresh lemon juice
1 teaspoon Dijon mustard
1/2 teaspoon garlic, minced
3/4 cup mayonnaise
salt and pepper to taste
dash of Tabasco

Mix all ingredients. Cover,
and refrigerate until serving time.

Garnish:

lemon wedges

Sam's "Local Boy" Cioppino

Serves 4

One of the good things about this recipe is that you can use just about any seafood. I've used the ones I like best, but it's really up to you. These are some of the seafood alternatives: scallops (bay or halved sea scallops), crab, red snapper, halibut, sea bass, striped bass, small clams, mussels, scrod, monkfish, squid (calamari), or medium to large shrimp.

1-1/2 pounds firm white fish
   (mahimahi, 'ahi, or ono),
   cut into large cubes
1/2 pound medium shrimp
1/2 cup light olive oil, for frying
1 Maui (sweet) onion, thinly sliced
1 cup celery, thinly sliced
1 cup bell peppers
   (assorted colors), julienned
1 tablespoon fresh garlic, minced
1 tablespoon fresh ginger, minced
2 tomatoes, diced
   1 cup white wine

juice of 1 fresh lemon
4 cups clam juice
5 cups water
1/2 teaspoon sambal oelek
   (chili paste)
1/4 cup fresh basil,
   chopped
pinch saffron
1 cup taro, steamed and
   cut into 1/2-inch cubes
1 cup sweet potato, steamed and
   cut into 1/2-inch cubes
1/2 pound clams or mussels
salt and pepper to taste

Garnish:

green onions, minced

Cut fish into 1-inch cubes.
Remove shells and devein shrimp.

In a large pan, sauté onions, celery, bell peppers, olive oil, garlic, and ginger. Add tomato and white wine. Simmer until wine is reduced by 1/4. Add lemon juice, clam juice, water, sambal oelek, basil, and saffron. Bring to a boil, then simmer for about 20 minutes.

Add cooked taro, sweet potatoes, and seafood. Cook for about 8 minutes or until the fresh clams open. Season with salt and pepper to taste.

Garnish with minced green onions.

> This type of fish stew, cioppino, is indigenous to Genoa, Italy, and named after a shellfish called ciuppino, enjoyed in Italy's Ligurian region. It's delicious and versatile, and can be made with a wide variety of fish and shellfish, limited only by availability, taste, and budget. Cioppino is ideal for a large dinner party or buffet, but it works for smaller gatherings, too.

Bowl provided by Faith Ogawa of Faith and Friends, Kamuela, Big Island; salt and pepper shaker lent by Rick Clark of Hawaiiana Vintage Collector, Kailua-Kona, Big Island; fabric by Hina Lei Creations, Kamuela, Big Island; napkin ring by Pi'i Laeha, Laupahoehoe, Big Island; napkin lent by Under the Koa Tree, King's Shop at the Waikoloa Resort, Big Island.

Crab Omelette

Serves I

There are many different types of omelettes—there is the French omelette, where the egg is beaten, then cooked in a thin sheet and stuffed; and the "puffy" omelette, where egg whites are beaten until frothy, then cooked to make a thick, but airy wrap for your filling. In the recipe on this page, the filling is mixed into the egg batter, and cooked as one very tasty egg pancake.

I demonstrated these Crab Omelettes on my show, and got a great response. I thought I'd share them with you here. I think that the garnish of green onions and tomatoes is just as important to the overall flavor of this dish as any of the other ingredients.

2 tablespoons light olive oil
1/2 cup mixed fresh vegetables, julienned
1/2 teaspoon fresh garlic, minced

1 tablespoon green onion, chopped
1/3 cup crab meat
2 large eggs, beaten
salt and pepper to taste

Heat oil in non-stick omelette pan. Sauté fresh vegetables and garlic in hot oil for 30 seconds. Salt and pepper to taste. Add green onion and crab meat. Cook for 45 seconds or until hot. Stir in beaten eggs, and cook over medium heat for 20 to 30 seconds. Flip omelette once to cook the top side. Fold in half, place on serving plate, and garnish with green onion and tomatoes. Serve immediately.

Garnish:

1 tablespoon green onion, chopped
2 tablespoons tomato, diced

GOSSAMER BAY
VINEYARDS
CALIFORNIA
WHITE ZINFANDEL
1995

ALC. 8% BY VOL.

Wok-Seared Ama Ebi
with Lemon Grass

Serves 4

On those "north wind" days, when it's really cold outside, try making this wok-seared ama ebi with lemon grass. The aroma alone will make you feel warm inside.

12 fresh ama ebi (extra-large
    jumbo shrimp)
4 tablespoons peanut oil
1 cup sugar snap peas,
    cut lengthwise in half
1 cup carrots, sliced

1 cup fresh straw mushrooms
1 cup fresh water chestnuts, sliced
Lemon Grass Broth
    (see recipe below)
salt and pepper to taste

Water chestnuts—the tubers of a marsh plant—have a pleasingly crisp texture and a mildly sweet flavor. You can find them canned in the Oriental foods section of the grocery store, or the fresh produce sections in some Oriental markets.

Heat 4 tablespoons of peanut oil, and sear the shrimp. Remove shrimp from wok pan, and set aside. Drain excess oil from pan, and add sugar snap peas, carrots, straw mushrooms, and water chestnuts. Stir-fry for 30 seconds. Add Lemon Grass Broth, and simmer for 45 seconds. Add shrimp, and simmer for 45 seconds more. Season with salt and pepper. Divide into 4 pasta bowls, arranging shrimp on top. Garnish with daikon sprouts. Serve immediately.

Lemon Grass Broth:

1 fresh Hawaiian chili pepper, minced
2 stalks lemon grass, bias cut
1 clove fresh garlic, chopped
2 tablespoons fresh ginger, chopped
1 kaffir lime leaf
1 sprig fresh tarragon (optional)
1 tablespoon peanut oil
3 cups chicken stock

In a hot wok, sear chili pepper, lemon grass, garlic, ginger, lime leaf, and tarragon in 1 tablespoon peanut oil. Add chicken stock. Let simmer for 10 to 15 minutes.

Garnish:

1 package daikon sprouts

Seafood Creole

Serves 4

This is one of my favorite fish stews. I love the spicy broth and the sheer quantity of the seafood. I like the seafood meat cut into large chunks so that I can really taste the individual flavors.

2 tablespoons light olive oil
1 large onion, chopped
1 celery stalk, chopped
1 green bell pepper, chopped
3 cloves fresh garlic, minced
1 teaspoon ground cumin
1 teaspoon fresh thyme leaves, chopped
1 bay leaf
1 medium tomato, coarsely chopped
6 cups water or chicken broth

1/4 cup tomato paste
1/2 teaspoon sambal oelek (chili paste)
salt and pepper to taste
1 pound onaga (red snapper) fillets, with skin, cut in 2-inch pieces
8 pieces medium shrimp
12 pieces clams
8 pieces mussels
8 pieces scallops
3 cups rice, uncooked
1/4 cup cilantro, chopped

In a large skillet, heat oil; cook onion, celery, green pepper, and garlic until crisp-tender. Add cumin, thyme, bay leaf, and tomatoes, and sauté.

Add water, tomato paste, and sambal oelek (chili paste), and salt and pepper to taste. Bring to a boil; reduce heat, and simmer covered for 10 minutes. Add seafood, and cook until the clam shells open: about 8 minutes. Remove the seafood, set aside.

Add rice, and cover and simmer for about 30 minutes. Turn off heat, and allow to sit for 15 minutes, covered. Fold in chopped cilantro, place in a bowl, and top with seafood mixture. Serve hot. Garnish with cilantro.

Garnish:

4 whole-leaf cilantro sprigs

Snappers are common on shallow tropical reefs throughout the world. Most snappers native to Hawai'i inhabit depths greater than 200 feet. These include 'opakapaka, 'ula'ula, and onaga, some of the Islands' best-loved food fishes.

Ceramic Bowl made by Ed Enomoto, Kula, Maui; Flowers donated by Alice, Ichiro, and Deedee Yamaguchi, Kamuela, Big Island.

Oven-Roasted Dungeness Crab
with Garlic Butter

Serves 4

Dungeness crab meat is sweet, delicate, and flaky. Since the crab is large, the meat is relatively easy to dig out. It's very popular just about anywhere. Dungeness crabs are sold alive, cooked whole, and as fresh canned meat. (This is unlike the other large crabs— the king and snow crabs—which are available frozen year round.)

I love Dungeness crab, so I wanted to include a recipe that showcased the simple elegance of this seafood. Garlic, butter, cilantro, lemon—who could want for more?

1/4 pound butter, softened
2 tablespoons fresh garlic, chopped
1 tablespoon fresh cilantro, chopped
1 teaspoon pepper flakes

juice from 1 fresh lemon
salt and pepper to taste
1 large Dungeness crab,
   cleaned, gills removed

Mix butter, garlic, cilantro, pepper flakes, lemon juice, salt, and pepper. Pack stuffing into crab (under shell and around). Place crab into a baking pan. Cover with foil, and bake at 375° for about 15 minutes.

Lobster Club
with Tango Lettuce

Serves 1

The general Hawaiian name for the Hawaiian red lobster is "ula." There are a number of varieties of lobster that were given specific names in Hawai'i—hiwa (entirely black), koa'e, poni (a purple-like color), 'apa'apa'a, hawa'ewa'e (small).

There may not be a time you feel like making such a unique sandwich, but if the feeling arises to create something extravagant and great-tasting, try this lobster club. It will send you hunting for lobster so you can do it again.

5 ounces cooked lobster meat
3 sweet bread slices
1 tomato, sliced

1 head tango lettuce
4 slices bacon, cooked

Chop 3 ounces of the lobster meat; mix with sun-dried tomato-mayonnaise. Spread 1/2 of the mixture on 1 slice of sweet bread, and top with sliced tomato and lettuce. Top with another slice of sweet bread. Spread on the rest of the mayo/lobster mixture and top with lettuce, bacon, remaining 2 ounces of lobster meat and third slice of bread.

For Spread:

2 tablespoons sun-dried
   tomato, chopped
4 tablespoons mayonnaise

Combine chopped sun-dried tomatoes with 4 tablespoons of mayonnaise for spread, and set aside.

Panko Oysters
with Spicy, Vine-Ripened Tomato Relish

Serves 4

I recommend that you garnish these tasty oysters with furikake and lemon wedges. I wanted to use ogo in the Tomato Relish, but the furikake supplied the seaweed flavor. This one is 'ono.

24 large oysters, shucked and cleaned	2 cups vegetable oil, for deep-frying
1 cup all-purpose flour	salt and pepper to taste
3 whole eggs, beaten	Spicy, Vine-Ripened Tomato Relish (see recipe below)
3 cups panko (Japanese-style crispy bread crumbs)	Hijimi Rémoulade (see recipe below)

Furikake is a Japanese condiment made of seaweeds and sesame seeds. There are many different types on the market, some with dried-ground shrimp, fish, and other shellfish and seasonings. The furikake gives the rémoulade an interesting seaweed flavor.

Coat oysters in flour, egg, then panko. Deep-fry in oil until golden brown. Spread Spicy, Vine-Ripened Tomato Relish on the bottom of a serving platter. Arrange the deep-fried oysters over tomato relish, and sprinkle with furikake. Serve immediately with Hijimi Rémoulade on the side.

Spicy, Vine-Ripened Tomato Relish:

3 large vine-ripened tomatoes
1 medium Maui (sweet) onion, diced
1/2 green onion, chopped
1 Hawaiian chili pepper, minced
1/2 cup yellow pepper
1 teaspoon fresh garlic, minced
Hawaiian salt

Mix all ingredients together, and set aside.

Garnish:

aji nori furikake (dried seaweed flakes)
lemon wedges

Hijimi Rémoulade:

1 cup mayonnaise
1 teaspoon hijimi (spicy Japanese pepper sprinkle)
1 teaspoon garlic, chopped
1 tablespoon green onion, chopped
1 teaspoon furikake (dried seaweed flakes)
1 teaspoon lemon juice
2 tablespoons water

Blend all ingredients. Serve at room temperature.

Steamed Clams
in Asian Broth

Serves 4

To me, the main ingredient in this recipe is the lemon grass. It lends a delicate citrus flavor to the Manila clams. You can substitute any clams for the Manila ones. The recipe will work fine. I just prefer Manila clams with this ingredient combination.

4 pounds Manila clams
1/4 cup lemon grass,
   cut into thin diagonal slices
1/4 cup ginger, julienned
1 medium onion, julienned
2 tablespoons Aloha shoyu
1/4 teaspoon chili flakes

4 cups chicken stock
1/4 teaspoon garlic, minced
1/4 cup white wine
2 teaspoons sesame oil
salt and pepper to taste

Wash clams, and set aside. Place the rest of the ingredients in a pot, and bring to a boil. Let simmer for 10 minutes. Add clams, cover and bring back to a boil. Cook until clams open. Remove from heat, and serve in a soup tureen. Garnish with cilantro leaves.

Garnish:

cilantro leaves

Lemon grass is a favorite Southeast Asian herb. Citrus-scented, lemon grass adds distinctive flavor and aroma to the cooking of Indonesia, Malaysia, Indochina, and Thailand. It's occasionally sold fresh in Oriental markets, but you're more likely to find it frozen (in whole stalks) and dried.

Bowl made by R. Jeff Lee of Lee Ceramics, Waialua, O'ahu; flowers donated by Momi Greene of Greene Acres, Kailua-Kona, Big Island.

Seared Ginger Scallops
with Tomato-Chanterelles Lomi

Serves 4

Sea scallops are almost always shucked on board ship because they die quickly once out of the water. These large scallops are farmed in the waters off Japan and British Columbia. Similar scallops—the Pacific sea and weathervane scallops —are brought into Hawai'i from the Pacific Northwest.

The contrast of the deep red tomatoes and brown mushrooms with the white scallops on top, laced with the chopped green onion, makes this a very elegant dish.

4 tablespoons all-purpose flour
salt and pepper to taste
1/2 tablespoon sesame seeds
1 teaspoon ginger powder

20 sea scallops
2 tablespoons light olive oil
Tomato-Chanterelles Lomi
   (see recipe below)

Make Tomato-Chanterelles Lomi, and set aside.

Mix flour with salt, pepper, sesame seeds, and ginger powder in a shallow bowl. Roll the scallops in flour mixture. In a large sauté pan, sear scallops in oil for 1 minute on each side over high heat. Remove scallops from pan, and rinse. Place scallops on Tomato-Chanterelles Lomi, and garnish with green onions.

Tomato-Chanterelles Lomi:

1 cup fresh chanterelle mushrooms, sliced
1/2 cup Maui (sweet) onion, sliced
1 teaspoon fresh ginger, chopped
1/2 cup fresh scallion, chopped
2 medium tomatoes, diced
3 tablespoons Aloha shoyu
2 tablespoons light olive oil
2 tablespoons chicken stock
1 teaspoon Dijon mustard
1 tablespoon rice vinegar
2 tablespoons sesame oil
salt and pepper to taste

Heat wok with 2 tablespoons of olive oil. Stir-fry the chanterelles, Maui onion, and ginger for 1 minute. Add the rest of the ingredients, and salt and pepper to taste. Cook for 1 to 2 minutes, and set aside.

Garnish:

2 tablespoons green onions, chopped

Steamed Clams
with Ginger Pesto Butter

Serves 4

When purchasing "live" clams, make sure all of the shells are closed. If they are open, the clams are dead. Do not eat them. If the clams are frozen, they are sometimes open. If they were previously frozen, and open, it's OK. But if you're buying them fresh, they should all be closed.

24 fresh steamer clams
1 medium round onion, thinly sliced
1/2 teaspoon fresh garlic, chopped
3 cups chicken stock
1 cup fresh shiitake mushrooms, julienned

2 cups mustard cabbage, julienned
1 tablespoon green onion, chopped
salt and pepper to taste
4 tablespoons Ginger Pesto Butter (see recipe below)

Rinse fresh clams to ensure that clam shells are closed.

Place clams, onions, garlic, and chicken stock in a small pot. Steam for 1 minute. Add all vegetables, and cook for 2 to 3 minutes. Salt and pepper to taste, then remove from stove.

Divide clams into 4 serving bowls. Dollop each serving with 1 tablespoon Ginger Pesto Butter. Garnish with cilantro leaves, and serve immediately.

Ginger Pesto Butter:

4 ounces fresh ginger
1 ounce fresh garlic
1 cup light olive oil
1/4 cup fresh cilantro
1/2 cup green onion
salt and pepper to taste
1/4 pound butter, softened

Blend all ingredients in a blender.

Garnish:

4 sprigs fresh cilantro leaves

Mustard cabbage—bok choy, sometimes called Chinese mustard cabbage—is elongated, and unfurls dark-green leaves from long white stalks. Choose heads with smooth white stalks and crisp, unblemished leaves. This leafy vegetable can be refrigerated for up to 4 days if stored in a plastic bag.

ECCO DOMANI
ITALIAN WHITE WINE

— 1996 —
PINOT GRIGIO
DELLE
VENEZIE
INDICAZIONE GEOGRAFICA TIPICA
IMPORTED BY ECCO DOMANI USA, INC, SANTA ROSA CA. ALC. 12% BY VOL.

Coconut Mac-Nut Shrimp
with Guava Sweet & Sour Sauce

Serves 4

Now, this is a tasty treat. I love dishes that blend a variety of textures, flavors, and aromas. This one is a real winner. Adding the coconut flakes makes all the difference. They crisp up into spiny-looking prongs that crackle when you bite into them. You'll love this one.

1 cup coconut flakes
1 cup roasted macadamia nuts, crushed
2-1/2 cups panko (Japanese-style crispy bread crumbs)
1 cup all-purpose flour

24 pieces shrimp (21-25 pieces per pound)
3 or 4 whole eggs, whipped
4 cups vegetable oil
salt and pepper to taste
Sam Choy's Guava Sweet & Sour Sauce (see recipe below)

Just a little note about thickening. Be sure to bring your sauce to a boil before adding the cornstarch, and cook for 1 to 2 minutes. Otherwise the sauce may retain an unpleasant starchy taste. (The amount of cornstarch in my recipes is just a suggestion; you may want to add more for a thicker sauce. But be careful. A little cornstarch goes a long way.)

Mix coconut flakes, macadamia nuts, and panko together. Bread the shrimp in flour, egg, and then in coconut flake-macadamia nut-panko mixture. Season with salt and pepper. Deep-fry until golden brown. Serve with Sam Choy's Guava Sweet & Sour Sauce.

Sam Choy's Guava Sweet & Sour Sauce:

1/2 cup ketchup
1/2 cup white wine vinegar
1/2 cup water
2 teaspoons Aloha shoyu
1/2 cup granulated sugar
1/4 cup frozen guava concentrate, undiluted
1-1/2 teaspoons fresh garlic, minced
1/4 teaspoon hot pepper sauce
1/4 cup pineapple juice
4 tablespoons cornstarch mixed with 3 tablespoons water, for thickening

In a medium saucepan, combine all sweet and sour ingredients except cornstarch mixture. Blend well, bring to a boil, then add cornstarch mixture. Reduce heat and simmer, stirring frequently until thickened.

GOSSAMER BAY
VINEYARDS
CALIFORNIA
WHITE ZINFANDEL
1995
ALC 8% BY VOL.

Papier-mâché background by Terry Taube, Kailua-Kona, Big Island; square ceramic platter lent by Hilton Waikoloa Village, Waikoloa, Big Island; Carrot flower carving donated by Raymond M. Yamasaki of Ray's Oriental Designs, Kamuela, Big Island; sauce container by Georgia Sartoris of Georgia Sartoris Fine Art, Pa'auilo, Big Island; flowers donated by James McCully Orchid Culture, Hakalau, Big Island

Steamed Maryland Blue Crabs

Serves 4

Blue crab is found in the Atlantic from Cape Cod to Florida, and in the Gulf of Mexico. It has also been introduced to the Mediterranean. This blue crab has a sweet taste and flaky meat. Whole Maryland crabs can be purchased live or cooked, with a hard or soft shell.

Don't be neat with this meal. Spread a thick layer of newspapers on your table and pound away! When you're done, just roll up the papers and toss them in the garbage. You can use just about any type of medium crab with this recipe. They will all taste great.

12 live Maryland Blue crabs	Beer (optional)
1-1/2 cups Old Bay seasoning	Drawn butter (optional)
1/8 cup cayenne powder	

Rinse crabs in cold running water. Bring water (or water and beer) to boil in bottom of steamer. Carefully drop crabs into upper section of steamer. Sprinkle Old Bay and cayenne powder on top of crabs. Cover, and steam for 20 minutes.

Place the crabs on a big platter. When cool enough to handle, crack with a hammer, and pick the meat. Meat can be rubbed in a little of the seasoning mix that has fallen onto the tray and/or dipped in drawn butter.

Great served with steamed white corn on the cob and onion rings.

Steamed "'Ono-licious" Shrimp

Serves 3–4

I've included quite a few shrimp recipes in this seafood cookbook because shrimp are so very versatile, and because I like them so much. This has got to be one of my favorites. I've demonstrated it on my television show, and thought you might like to have it in my book. Enjoy!

12 pieces of fresh shrimp,
   21-25 pieces per pound
1/2 cup sherry
salt and white pepper to taste
1 whole egg
1 teaspoon cornstarch

1/2 cup smoked ham (preferrably
   Farmer John ham), diced
1/2 cup green onion, minced
1 or 2 slices fresh ginger, minced
2 tablespoons round onion, minced
1/2 teaspoon granulated sugar

Marinate shrimp in sherry, salt, and white pepper for 1 hour. Discard marinade. Add the egg and 1 teaspoon cornstarch to shrimp, and massage to coat. Arrange shrimp mixture in a dish. Place the dish into a steamer, and sprinkle with ham, green onion, ginger, and round onion. Season with sugar, and steam until done (about 15 minutes).

The type of steamer doesn't matter. It's the steam and/or the liquid in the pot (save a rack and a tight-fitting lid) that does the cooking. If you don't have a steamer, just cut out the tops and bottoms of three or four tuna (or similar-sized) cans, place them in the bottom of a large soup pot, a rack or tray or heatproof platter. Add the steaming liquid or water to the bottom of the pot, bring the water to a boil, and you're in business.

Scallops
with Chinese Cabbage and Ramen

Serves 4

> *Our experience with scallops is strange. Since we eat only the muscle and rarely see scallops in their beautiful shells, we see the shell and seafood as two separate things—the one, a crimped, pretty shell found on beaches, and the other, a round, white bit of meat found in seafood shops.*

Usually, when I'm making a stir fry dish like this, I like to have my ingredients in some sort of uniform size. So, I would probably use whole small scallops, and quarter large ones. That way, the sauce permeates the scallops faster.

2 tablespoons vegetable oil
20 ounces scallops
2 tablespoons Aloha shoyu
2 teaspoons ginger, minced
1/4 teaspoon garlic, minced
1-1/2 tablespoons assorted Chinese cabbage, cut into 1-inch cubes

2 tablespoons oyster sauce
1 teaspoon sesame oil
2 pounds precooked ramen or Asian noodles
1 cup chicken stock
salt and pepper to taste

Heat vegetable oil in a teflon wok pan over high heat. Add scallops and shoyu. Stir-fry for 2 minutes. Add ginger and garlic, and cook for 30 seconds more. Remove scallops from wok, and set aside. Place Chinese cabbage, oyster sauce, and sesame oil in wok, and cook for 2 to 3 minutes. Add the ramen and chicken stock. Season with salt and pepper. Cook for 3 minutes, then remove from heat. Place seasoned noodles on a platter, and top with scallops. Serve immediately.

Ceramic platter lent by Hilton Waikoloa Village, Waikoloa, Big Island; Pipipi shell lei lent by Patrick Choy, Honolulu, O'ahu.

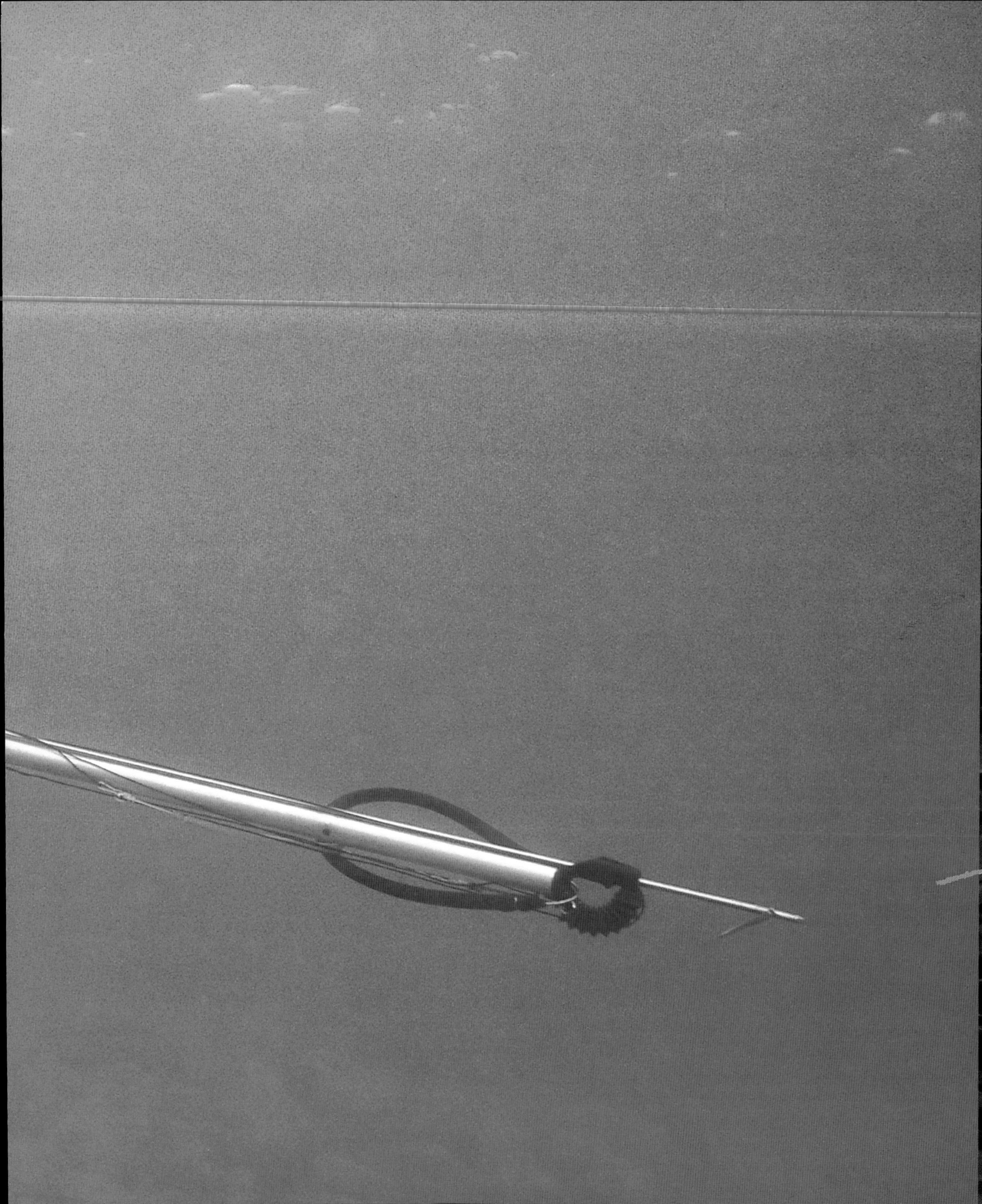

SIX

BARBECUE

Spearfishing

For fishermen who prefer being in the water with their prey, for actually seeing their potential catch and swimming after it, there is only spearfishing. It's fascinating and fun working the reefs underwater. You learn so much about the fish and their domain. You become a part of it.

I spent a lot of time as a kid just snorkeling in the ocean around La'ie, and I'll tell you, anyone thinking of taking up spearfishing should make a lot of scouting trips through the reefs before you grab a spear. It's good to have a sense of your surroundings, understand how light angles in at certain times of day and certain depths, see where the fish hide and how they respond to you, and feel the surge of the water—the currents and swells.

A lot of local spearfishermen go out alone, but I would recommend a buddy. You're in the wilderness out there, with eels, sharks, sea snakes, sharp coral and urchins. Having a friend around could save your life.

Diving the reefs along Windward O'ahu or the Kona Coast has to be one of the greatest experiences. This might sound strange, but I believe my fishing adventures—especially the spearfishing—make me a better seafood chef. Witnessing the cycles of the fish, you know—what they eat and where they swim, how their fat content changes with seasons and water temperature—all this knowledge goes into how I prepare my seafood.

There is so much beauty under the surface. Watching the limu ripple with the surge, hearing the clicking of the mollusks, and seeing schools of fish swirl with all their colors through the sunlight, I know this is Mother Nature at her best. And spearfishing is so visual and immediate, not like blindly casting a hook into a body of blue ocean and hoping to snag whatever takes the bait. Underwater, you experience the sense of discovery, of spotting that perfect fish and moving in for the shot, taking only what you want—that big bright uhu or champion kala, a prize for your hungry family.

Barbecued A'u (Swordfish) Kabobs

Serves 4

I made life easier for you by bottling my "Original Oriental Creamy Dressing."
I also included the recipe here for those folks who want to make it from scratch.
Use the bottled dressing or make it yourself, it's up to you. There's information
at the back of the book on how to order the dressing, or you can pick it up from
your local grocery store.

A'u (swordfish) is a moderately oily, very flavorful fish with a firm, meat-like texture. The a'u can grow to be huge—weighing sometimes more than half a ton. Although the meat's oily nature makes it a perfect fish for the hibachi, if overcooked, the fillets will turn dry and tough.

24 ounces a'u (swordfish or marlin)
  meat, cut into 1 inch cubes
1 tablespoon peanut oil
24 mushrooms
1 length of Portuguese sausage,
  cut into 24 equal pieces

salt and pepper to taste
3/4 cup Sam Choy's Original
  Oriental Creamy Dressing
  (see recipe below)

Marinate fish in Sam Choy's Original Oriental Creamy Dressing for about 20
minutes. Arrange on 4 skewers alternately: first a cube of fish, then a piece of
sausage, then a mushroom, and repeat.

Grill on a hot charcoal fire for about 10 minutes; time depends on heat and
distance from fire. Let dripping sausage flame up to sear the fish, then move
skewers around the top of the grill to avoid burning. Skewer can be rotated after
the sausage adheres to the cubes of fish. Garnish with chopped cilantro, and
serve with Sam Choy's Original Oriental Creamy Dressing on the side.

**Sam Choy's Original Oriental
Creamy Dressing:**

3 cups mayonnaise
1/2 cup Aloha shoyu
3/4 cup granulated sugar
1/4 teaspoon white pepper
1-1/2 tablespoons black goma
  (black sesame seeds)
1 tablespoon sesame oil
2 tablespoons water

Whisk all ingredients together until well
blended.

Garnish:

fresh cilantro, finely chopped

Broiled Lobster
with Basil-Garlic Butter Sauce and Grilled Corn Relish

Serves 1–2

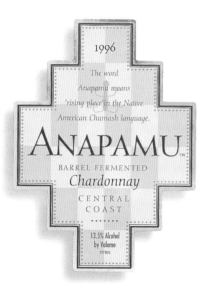

Many local grocery stores have fish and meat sections that display live Maine lobsters swimming in tanks. These delicious, hard-shelled creatures are categorized and priced in three sizes. Most weigh about 1-1/4 pounds, and each one is considered a single portion. Large lobsters weigh more than 1-1/2 pounds. And extra-large lobsters weigh 2-1/4 pounds or more.

Lobsters are great for barbecues because they come in their own self-contained package. Just throw them over the coals, cover the grill, and let them cook, or broil them in the oven. The meat stays quite moist, protected by the hard shell. They're traditionally served with butter, but adding a little basil is just the perfect touch to spice up the flavor.

1-1/2 pounds fresh, live Maine lobster
salt and pepper to taste

Basil Garlic Sauce (see recipe below)
Grilled Corn Relish (see recipe below)

Cut lobster in half, season with salt and pepper, and broil until cooked.

To serve, place lobster on a platter, and drizzle with Basil-Garlic Butter Sauce, or serve Basil-Garlic Butter Sauce in ramikin dish on the side for dipping. Garnish lobster with lemon wedges, and serve with Grilled Corn Relish.

Basil-Garlic Butter Sauce:

6 tablespoons butter, softened
2 teaspoons fresh garlic, puréed
1 tablespoon fresh basil, minced
juice of 1/2 fresh lemon
salt and pepper to taste

Heat butter, and add the rest of the ingredients, except basil. Cook until garlic is translucent. Add basil and cook for 30 seconds.

Garnish:

4 lemon wedges

Grilled Corn Relish:

1/2 onion, chopped
1/2 cup red pepper, chopped
2 tablespoons light olive oil
1 teaspoon garlic, minced
3 corn cobs, grilled then shucked
salt and pepper to taste
1/4 cup cilantro, chopped coarsely

Sauté the onions and pepper with olive oil. Add garlic and grilled corn kernels. Add salt and pepper to taste. Fold in cilantro.

1996
The word Anapamu means 'rising place' in the Native American Chumash language.

ANAPAMU
BARREL FERMENTED
Chardonnay
CENTRAL COAST
13.5% Alcohol by Volume

Fluted koa platter piece by Gerald Ben, artwork provided by Chesnut & Company, Holualoa, Big Island; antique tapa lent by Mindy Raymond; etched gourd made by Momi Greene of Greene Acres, Kailua-Kona, Big Island.

Creole Grilled Onaga

Serves 6

Onaga is the Japanese name for red snapper. The Hawaiians called this fish 'ula'ula, meaning red-red, describing the color of the red snapper's skin. The flesh of these and all snappers is white to pinkish white, with very few bones. 'Ula'ula was sometimes used as a sacrificial offering when a red fish was required.

Your grill size depends on the size of the onaga you have. I like cooking them all at once. I've included a recipe for Creole Seasoning Mix. This will stay fresh in your refrigerator for weeks, and it's great for use in chicken dishes.

6 tablespoons butter, melted
3 tablespoons onion, chopped
1/4 cup green bell pepper, chopped
1/4 cup fresh cilantro, minced
1 tablespoon chili garlic sauce

1/4 cup round onion, chopped
2 tablespoons Creole Seasoning Mix
  (see recipe below)
1 6-pound whole onaga
  (red snapper)

Combine butter, onion, bell pepper, cilantro, chili garlic sauce, and Creole Seasoning Mix in a saucepan. Place onaga on a sheet of heavy foil, and cover with butter sauce. Seal the foil using double folds to ensure there are no leaks. Place foil bundle on grill, and cover with grill cover. Cook for 20 to 30 minutes, and turn every 10 minutes, being careful not to tear the foil. Open foil, drain, and reserve liquid. Cook another 10 minutes, basting with the liquid.

Place fish on platter. Drizzle with basting sauce, and top with lemon slices.

Creole Seasoning Mix:

1 teaspoon salt
1 teaspoon white pepper
3/4 teaspoon ground cayenne pepper
3/4 teaspoon black pepper
1/2 teaspoon onion salt
1/2 teaspoon fresh thyme leaves
1/4 teaspoon fresh oregano leaves

Combine all ingredients in a small bowl. Store in an air-tight container.

Garnish:

2 lemons, sliced

Foil-Wrapped 'Opelu

Serves 6

This is a great way to cook fish, any small fish, over a hot grill. The stuffing seasons the meat, while the foil wrapping keeps it moist. It's really fun to make as a camping dinner. Throw some unhusked Kahuku corn on the barbecue, too, and wait for the raves.

6 small 'opelu, pan-dressed, skinned,
  between 6 to 8 ounces each

Cut 6 squares of heavy-duty aluminum foil, 18 inches each. Grease lightly with vegetable oil. Place one 'opelu on half of each foil square.

Whisk sauce ingredients in a bowl. Divide sauce among (and pour on) each of the 6 fish. Seal foil edges by making double folds. Place packages on a barbecue grill about 6 inches from moderately hot coals. Cook for 15 to 20 minutes or until done.

To serve, cut a big crisscross in the top of each package, and fold the foil back.

Sauce:

1 cup dry white wine
1/2 cup vegetable oil
1/2 cup fresh mushrooms, chopped
1/4 cup green onion, chopped
2 tablespoons fresh lemon juice
2 tablespoons fresh cilantro, chopped
2 teaspoons salt
1/2 teaspoon fresh thyme, minced
1/4 teaspoon bay leaf, crushed
1/4 teaspoon black pepper

Blend, and set aside.

'Opelu is a mackerel scad with very fine scales. In Hawaiian legend, this fish is associated with the coming of Pa'ao, an extremely influential high priest, to Hawai'i from the ancient land of Kahiki. In ancient times, 'opelu were abundant off the coast of Ka'u, on the Big Island. Offerings were left at a heiau (temple) in Ka'u to ensure a successful catch.

Grilled Marinated Mahimahi
with Poha, Mango, and Papaya Relish

Serves 4

I like to start the coals going, then make the Poha, Mango, and Papaya Relish, and put it in the refrigerator. Then comes the marinade, and we're on our way. This is a very easy, very elegant dish that tastes wonderful.

4 mahimahi fillets, 6 ounces each
Mahimahi Marinade
  (see recipe below)

4 cups organic greens
Poha, Mango, and Papaya Relish
  (see recipe below)

Most of the nation's mahimahi are harvested off the coasts of Hawai'i and Florida. During warmer periods, mahimahi have been snared in areas along the Pacific coast from Southern California to South America, and on the east coast as far north as Long Island.

Marinate mahimahi for 10 minutes. Grill over medium coals for 2 to 3 minutes on each side. Remove from heat, and place on a platter over organic greens. Serve with Poha, Mango, and Papaya Relish on the side.

Mahimahi Marinade:

1/2 cup macadamia nuts, crushed
1/2 cup Aloha shoyu
2 tablespoons honey
1/4 cup granulated sugar

  Mix ingredients together until sugar is dissolved. Set aside.

Poha, Mango, and Papaya Relish:

1/4 cup mango, diced medium
1/4 cup papaya, diced medium
1/4 cup poha berries, cut in half
1/4 cup red pepper, diced small
2 tablespoons yellow onions, diced small
2 tablespoons cilantro, minced
1 tablespoon lime juice
2 tablespoons granulated sugar

  Mix all ingredients together, and chill for 1 hour before serving.

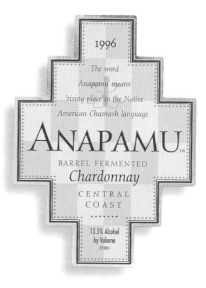

1996

The word Anapamu means 'rising place' in the Native American Chumash language.

ANAPAMU

BARREL FERMENTED
Chardonnay

CENTRAL COAST

13.5% Alcohol
by Volume

Plate provided by Liberty House; scarf provided by Liberty House-Kona; poha berries donated by Alice and Ichiro Yamaguchi, Kamuela, Big Island.

Calamari
with a Hibachi Twist

Serves 4

Calamari (true squid) come as perfect packages for stuffing. I love creating tasty fillings to go into their natural pouches. This is a very simple stuffing—some ginger, garlic, cilantro, shoyu, and butter. You know me, I really like simple stuff that tastes GREAT!

1-1/2 pounds small calamari, cleaned and skinned
1 sprig fresh cilantro, chopped
2 tablespoons fresh ginger, minced
2 tablespoons fresh garlic, minced

2 tablespoons Aloha shoyu
1 tablespoon butter, softened
salt and pepper to taste
2 tablespoons light olive oil

Cut off the calamari tentacles and chop them up. Mix them with the cilantro, ginger, garlic, shoyu, and butter. Stuff the bodies of the calamari with this mixture, and close the open ends with a wooden pick. Lightly score the sides of the stuffed calamari to allow for expansion during cooking. Season with salt and pepper, then brush with olive oil. Broil for 10 to 15 minutes, turning once.

Cilantro Salmon Steaks

Serves 6

Salmon steaks, 1-inch thick, will cook on your grill in about 10 minutes, allowing 5 minutes on each side. A 1-1/2-inch steak requires 7 minutes per side, and a 2-inch steak about 10 minutes per side. If baked or broiled in an oven, the necessary time is less, as the steaks cook on both sides at once. Test with a fork to see if it is done.

Old Hawaiians called salmon "kamano." This name was first given to the rainbow trout that were introduced into streams on Kaua'i. Salmon was later brought in, and given the name kamano. But this hardy Pacific Northwest Coast fish never could establish itself here in the subtropics.

1/2 cup rosé wine
1 tablespoon fresh cilantro, minced
2 tablespoons round onion, minced
1 teaspoon garlic
1/2 cup light olive oil
6 salmon steaks,
  each 1 to 2 inches thick

2 vine-ripened tomatoes,
  cut into wedges
1 Maui (sweet) onion,
  cut into wedges
Italian dressing of your choice
salt and pepper to taste

Combine the wine, cilantro, onion, garlic, and olive oil. Pour mixture over uncooked salmon in a shallow glass pan. The amounts of seasoning in the marinade can be increased to your taste. Use more marinade, if necessary, to cover the salmon steaks. Refrigerate for 1 hour, turning salmon once. Drain well. Broil fish. Serve with slices of vine-ripened tomatoes and Maui onions, drizzled with your favorite Italian dressing. Garnish with a sprinkling of chopped cilantro.

Garnish:

cilantro, chopped

'Ahi
with Lime-Shoyu Marinade

Serves 4

The lime juice in the "Lime-Shoyu Marinade" will "acid cook" the 'ahi fillets. It will also seal in the 'ahi juices, making the finished, grilled fish succulent and moist. I still caution to not overcook your fish.

'Ahi, like all fish, tends to dry out when cooked too long. To avoid turning a beautiful fillet into a tough chunk of meat, I marinate the fish, then cook it rather quickly. That way I lock in the flavors and fish's natural juices. I know I say it all the time, but DO NOT OVER-COOK your fish.

**4 'ahi (yellowfin tuna) fillets,
    6 ounces each**

Combine marinade ingredients, and marinate fish for 30 minutes, turning occasionally. Grill or broil fish for 5 to 6 minutes on each side, basting with marinade.

Do not overcook.

Lime-Shoyu Marinade:

1/4 cup Aloha shoyu
1/4 cup oil
juice and grated zest of 1 lime
2 tablespoons dry sherry
2 tablespoons cilantro, chopped
1 tablespoon fresh garlic, minced
1 tablespoon brown sugar
2 teaspoons fresh ginger, minced
1/8 teaspoon Chinese 5-Spice Powder

Blend ingredients, and set aside.

Broiled 'Opakapaka

Serves 4

'Opakapaka has mild-tasting, very tender, flaky meat. I've included some very intriguing flavors to accompany this fish—a combination of spicy, hot, aromatic, and tart, with the mellowing effect of a sweet, creamy dressing. It's a classic flavor blend from the new "Pacific Rim Cuisine."

4 fresh 'opakapaka fillets, about
   6 ounces each, boneless

Sam Choy's Original Creamy Oriental
   Dressing (see recipe below)
Hawaiian Salsa (see recipe below)

'Opakapaka, commonly known as crimson snapper or Hawaiian pink snapper, are usually caught at depths between 30 and 100 fathoms (or between 180 and 600 feet). They are found throughout the tropical Pacific, but the largest (weighing from 12 to 18 pounds) grow in waters off the Hawaiian Islands. These 'opakapaka are believed to be at least 10 years old.

Marinate 'opakapaka in 3 cups of Sam Choy's Original Creamy Oriental Dressing for 10 to 15 minutes. Remove from marinade and grill very quickly, about 3 to 4 minutes on both sides. Serve with Hawaiian Salsa, and garnish with cilantro.

Hawaiian Salsa:

1 large fresh pineapple, peeled,
   cored, and quartered
1 red bell pepper, finely diced
1 green bell pepper, finely diced
1 small red onion, finely diced
4 tablespoons light olive oil
3 tablespoons fresh cilantro, chopped
1 fresh lime juice
2 tablespoons fresh parsley, finely chopped
2 tablespoons fresh chives, finely chopped
1 fresh red chili, minced with seeds
1/2 avocado, not too ripe, diced (drizzle
   with lime juice to prevent browning)
salt and pepper to taste

Grill pineapple until almost brown, about 5 minutes per side. Chop finely. Mix with all remaining ingredients. Refrigerate until needed.

Sam Choy's Original Oriental Creamy Dressing:

3 cups mayonnaise
1/2 cup Aloha shoyu
3/4 cup granulated sugar
1/4 teaspoon white pepper
1-1/2 tablespoons black goma (black
   sesame seeds)
1 tablespoon sesame oil
2 tablespoons water

Whisk all ingredients together until well blended.

Garnish:

1 bunch fresh cilantro, chopped

Indigo Hills
1995
North Coast
SAUVIGNON BLANC

Grilled Mixed Seafood Salad

Serves 4

This recipe calls for shrimp, scallops, and fish. I didn't say exactly what kind because any sturdy white meat fish will do. Swordfish, ono, 'ōpakapaka, or 'ahi will all work just fine. My personal favorite is ono for this recipe.

12 pieces shrimp,
  peeled and deveined
12 pieces scallops
12 pieces fish, 1 ounce each

Seafood Marinade
  (see recipe below)
24 ounces organic greens
Spicy Citrus Dressing
  (see recipe below)

Marinate seafood for 10 minutes in Seafood Marinade. Grill over medium coals for 2 to 3 minutes. Place on platter over organic greens, and garnish with orange segments, crispy wonton, and tomato slices. Serve with Spicy Citrus Dressing.

Seafood Marinade:

1 cup Aloha shoyu
1 tablespoon oyster sauce
1 tablespoon sesame oil
1/2 cup brown sugar
1 tablespoon cilantro, chopped
1 teaspoon chili flakes
1 teaspoon garlic, minced
1/4 teaspoon Chinese 5-Spice Powder

Mix all ingredients until sugar is dissolved.

Garnish:

orange segments
deep-fried crispy wonton chips
yellow and red tomatoes, sliced

Spicy Citrus Dressing:

1/2 cup Aloha shoyu
1/2 cup cider vinegar
1/2 cup orange juice
2 tablespoons sesame oil
1/2 cup granulated sugar
1 teaspoon chili flakes
salt and pepper
  to taste

Mix ingredients together until sugar is dissolved.

Fried 'Opelu
with Tomato-Ogo Relish

Serves 4

'Opelu get to be about 16 inches in length with a slender, agile-looking body. Its coloring is remarkable. The upper part of this fish is silvery-blue, with a lighter shade below. There are many dark, broken crisscross streaks marking the upper body that fade off into spots as they move toward the belly.

'Opelu is a really delicious fish, and makes a beautiful presentation when fried whole. The meat is tender, and there aren't too many bones, but it's always a good idea to be careful when eating whole fish. Be sure to lightly flour the fish to seal in the flavor.

4 whole 'opelu, cleaned
salt and pepper to taste
1/2 cup all-purpose flour

vegetable oil, for pan-frying
Tomato-Ogo Relish
   (see recipe below)

Salt and pepper fish to taste. Dredge fish in flour. Shake off excess flour.

Heat oil in pan, and fry 'opelu at medium-high temperature for 3 to 4 minutes on each side until done.

Place fish on a platter, and serve with Tomato-Ogo Relish on the side.

Tomato-Ogo Relish:

2 medium, vine-ripened tomatoes, diced
1/2 Maui (sweet) onion, diced
1/4 cup green onion, chopped
1 cup ogo, coarsely chopped
1 tablespoon ginger, minced
1 teaspoon garlic, minced
1/2 cup Aloha shoyu
2 to 3 pieces Hawaiian chili pepper, minced
juice of 1/2 lemon

Mix together to blend.

Grilled Basil-Ginger A'u Steaks

Serves 6

I like to custom-fit each one of my marinades to the particular type of fish, using seasonings and aromatics that enhance the meat's flavor. If you want, you can mix and match the marinades to fit your own taste. I believe in individuality. Have fun with it.

Marinade (see recipe below)
6 a'u (marlin or swordfish) fillets,
  6 ounces each, 1-inch thick

Basil-Garlic Butter, melted
  (see recipe below)

There is a thing called the Canadian Rule that says to cook a fish 10 minutes for every inch of thickness. This seems to hold up really well, except for the very thin steaks or fillets. You need to start cooking the fish on a well-heated grill. Keep in mind that if the fish is cold it will take a bit longer to cook.

Combine marinade ingredients, mix thoroughly. Place a'u steaks in marinade. Turn once or twice to make certain the fillets are well coated, and refrigerate for 1 hour.

With the grill about 6 inches from the coals, grill the fillets, uncovered, for 8 to 12 minutes. Baste the fillets with remaining marinade.

Arrange fillets on a platter, and drizzle with melted Basil-Garlic Butter Sauce. Garnish with finely chopped parsley.

Marinade:

1/4 cup olive oil
juice of 1 lemon
2 tablespoons white wine
3 cloves fresh garlic, chopped fine
1/4 cup fresh basil, chopped
1 tablespoon fresh ginger, minced
1 tablespoon cracked black pepper
salt to taste
Basil-Garlic Butter Sauce, melted
  (see recipe at right)
fresh parsley, finely chopped

Basil-Garlic Butter Sauce:

6 tablespoons butter, softened
2 teaspoons fresh garlic, puréed
juice of 1/2 fresh lemon
salt and pepper to taste
1 tablespoon fresh basil leaves,
  cut into thin strips

Heat butter, and add the rest of the ingredients (except basil). Cook until garlic is translucent. Add basil, and cook for 30 seconds. Make 1 batch for the marinade, and another to pour over a'u steaks to serve.

Garnish:

fresh parsley, finely chopped

Mahimahi
with Cilantro Chutney

Serves 4

Mahimahi has a sweet but mildly pronounced flavor that can be made milder by trimming away the darker portions of meat. The meat is very lean, white, and tender, and is great baked, broiled, blackened, sautéed, or grilled. It's also great used in chowders and savory seafood stews.

Mahimahi can be purchased frozen, previously frozen, or fresh. The frozen fish is usually a little soggy, and doesn't hold up as well on the grill. I prefer using fresh ingredients in all cases.

4 mahimahi fillets, 6 ounces each, about 3/4-to 1-inch thick
3/4 teaspoon salt
1/4 teaspoon black pepper

1/4 cup butter, melted
1 tablespoon fresh cilantro, minced
1 tablespoon fresh lemon juice
Cilantro Chutney (see recipe below)

Sprinkle fillets with salt and pepper. Mix butter, cilantro, and lemon juice.

Grill fish about 4 inches from medium coals on covered grill. Grill for 10 to 15 minutes, turning once and brushing 2 or 3 times with butter mixture until fish flakes easily with fork. Serve with Cilantro Chutney, and garnish each fillet with fresh lemon wedges.

Cilantro Chutney:

1/3 cup fresh lemon juice
2 cups fresh cilantro, minced
1/2 cup fresh coconut, grated
1/2 cup green onion, finely chopped
1-1/2 tablespoons fresh ginger, minced
1 tablespoon sambal oelek (chili paste)
2 teaspoons granulated sugar
1 teaspoon ground cumin
salt and pepper to taste

Place ingredients in the food processor, and purée. Adjust seasoning with salt and pepper.

Garnish:

fresh lemon wedges

Marinated Shrimp, Scallops, and Mango Kabobs

Serves 6

Don't worry about the mango on the kabobs. The sugar in the juice will form a sweet crust around the fruit pieces, and will flavor the shrimp and scallops as well. It's like candy.

The mango, a native of India, has been cultivated for over 6,000 years. A relative of the pistachio and cashew, the mango tree grows in tropical climates to an average height of 50 feet. In Hawai'i, our mango season runs from late May through mid-July.

1/3 cup fresh lemon juice
1 tablespoon ground mustard
1 tablespoon light olive oil
1 teaspoon ground cumin
1 tablespoon fresh cilantro, minced
1/2 teaspoon salt
1/8 teaspoon paprika

1 pound fresh or frozen large raw
  shrimp, peeled and deveined
1 pound scallops, washed and
  drained
1 medium mango,
  cut into 1-inch pieces
Mango Chutney (see recipe below)

Mix lemon juice, mustard, olive oil, cumin, cilantro, salt, and paprika in shallow glass or plastic dish. Add shrimp and scallops; turn to coat with marinade. Cover, and refrigerate at least 1 hour.

Remove shrimp and scallops from marinade; reserve marinade. Thread shrimp, scallops, and mango alternately on each of six 15-inch metal skewers, leaving space between each. Cover, and grill kabobs for 10 minutes, about 5 to 6 inches over medium coals. Turn, and brush 2 or 3 times with marinade, until shrimp are pink. Garnish with lime wedges. Serve over rice with Mango Chutney.

Mango Chutney

1 quart green mango slices
1 tablespoon salt
1 pound raw sugar
1 cup rice vinegar
5 ounces raisins
1 small Hawaiian chili pepper, chopped
1 tablespoon fresh garlic, minced
1/4 cup fresh ginger, minced

Garnish:

fresh lime wedges

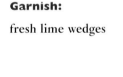

Combine mango slices and salt. Let stand overnight. Rinse and drain. Combine sugar and rice vinegar. Simmer for 30 minutes. Add mango slices and remaining ingredients. Simmer for 1 hour or until mangoes are tender, and chutney is of desired consistency. Makes about 1 quart.

Ono
with Grilled Garden Vegetables

Serves 4

This dish is a "for sure" winner. Just read the recipe. All of the red peppers, yellow squash, bright green asparagus, and mouth-watering grilled ono will make you hungry. The marinade works well with just about any fish, but it's my favorite for ono.

You know a fish tastes good when its Hawaiian name means "delicious." The ono, a close relative to the king mackerel, is also called a wahoo. It can grow to a weight of more than 100 pounds with a length of 5 to 6 feet. That's a lot of good eating. The usual size caught in Hawaiian waters ranges from 8 to 30 pounds.

4 ono fillets, 6 ounces each
Marinade (see recipe below)
1 zucchini or yellow squash,
   sliced oval
1 red bell pepper, cut into wedges
8 fresh shiitake mushrooms

1/2 pound asparagus,
   trim the bottom
1 piece medium carrot, sliced
1 medium Maui (sweet) onion, sliced
1/2 cup Sam Choy's Original
   Oriental Creamy Dressing
   (see recipe below)

Rub 1 tablespoon of marinade over each ono fillet. Let stand for 30 minutes.

Toss the vegetables with the remaining marinade, then grill over medium-high charcoals. Remove the vegetables, and place in the middle of a serving plate.

Grill fish over medium-high charcoals until cooked.

Serve with Sam Choy's Original Oriental Creamy Dressing on the side.

Marinade:

1 tablespoon fresh garlic, chopped
1/2 teaspoon black pepper
1 tablespoon sambal oelek (chili paste)
2 tablespoons fresh cilantro, chopped
1 tablespoon fresh thyme leaves
2 tablespoons white wine
3/4 cup salad oil
1 tablespoon sesame oil
1/4 cup Aloha shoyu
2 tablespoons oyster sauce

Mix ingredients together, and set aside.

Sam Choy's Original Oriental Creamy Dressing:

3 cups mayonnaise
1/2 cup Aloha shoyu
3/4 cup granulated sugar
1/4 teaspoon white pepper
1-1/2 tablespoons black goma
   (black sesame seeds)
1 tablespoon sesame oil
2 tablespoons water

Whisk all ingredients together until well blended.

Lava sculpture by Terry Taube, Kailua-Kona, Big Island; plate donated by Faith Ogawa, Kamuela, Big Island; fabric by Jan of Hina Lei Creations, Kamuela, Big Island; flowers provided by Roen Hufford, Kamuela, Big Island.

Poke Kabobs

Makes 6 kabobs

The Hawaiian word "poke" means to slice or cut crosswise into pieces. We use this term to describe our local raw fish and seafood serviche. I've taken it a little farther to describe the type of seasoning. This aʻu is seasoned with poke marinade, then skewered and put on the barbecue. It's so ʻono.

<table>
<tr><td>1 pound aʻu (marlin or swordfish),
   cut into twelve 1-1/4-inch cubes
12 cherry tomatoes
12 pieces round onion,
   1-1/4-inches each</td><td>4 fresh shiitake mushrooms,
   cut in quarters
Poke Marinade (see recipe below)
cooking spray</td></tr>
</table>

Soak fish cubes, cherry tomatoes, round onions, and shiitake mushrooms for 1 hour in Poke Marinade.

Place one fish cube, a shiitake mushroom quarter, a round onion piece, and a cherry tomato on each bamboo skewer, then repeat. Spray each kabob with cooking spray. Grill over medium-high coals until fish is medium rare. Enjoy!

Poke Marinade:

1/4 cup Aloha shoyu
1/2 cup ogo, chopped
1/4 cup green onion, chopped
1 tablespoon sesame oil

Mix shoyu, ogo, green onions, and sesame oil together to make a marinade.

The general term Hawaiians use for swordfish, marlin, and all other billed fish is aʻu. Like all of the large billfish (aʻu) caught by the ancient Hawaiians, the swordfish was feared because it could pierce a fishing canoe with its heavy bill.

Spicy Grilled Opah

Serves 4

Opah or moonfish has a sweet flavor that blends well with the spices used in this marinade and in the fruit chutney. Serve it up nice and hot with a couple scoops of rice. It's unreal.

4 opah, 6-ounce fillets

Pineapple Chutney
(see recipe below)

Mix marinade ingredients in shallow glass or plastic dish. Add fish; turn to coat with marinade. Cover, and refrigerate 1 hour.

Remove fish from marinade; reserve marinade. Cover, and grill fish for 10 to 15 minutes, about 4 inches from medium-high coals. Brush occasionally with marinade, and turn once.

Serve with Pineapple Chutney.

Opah or moonfish is one of the most colorful commercial fish species available in Hawai'i. A silvery-grey upper body shades to a rose red, dotted with white spots toward the belly. The fins of the opah are crimson, and its large eyes are encircled with gold. It's definitely a jewel of the ocean.

Marinade:

1/4 cup tomato juice
2 tablespoons fresh lemon juice
1 tablespoon dry sherry wine
2 tablespoons Aloha shoyu
2 tablespoons brown sugar
1 tablespoon light olive oil
1 tablespoon fresh ginger, minced
1/2 teaspoon ground cinnamon
1/2 teaspoon anise seed, crushed
1/4 teaspoon ground nutmeg
1/4 teaspoon ground cloves
1 tablespoon sambal oelek (chili paste)
salt to taste

Mix ingredients in mixing bowl, and set aside.

Pineapple Chutney:

2 cups fresh pineapple, chopped
1 cup raisins
1 tablespoon fresh ginger, finely chopped
1 tablespoon fresh garlic, finely chopped
1/2 tablespoon sambal oelek (chili paste)
1/2 cup rice vinegar
3/4 cup brown sugar
1/2 teaspoon ground cinnamon
1/2 teaspoon salt
1/2 cup macadamia nuts, chopped

Combine everything (except nuts) in a large saucepan, and cook slowly until pineapple is tender, about 30 minutes. Stir in nuts, and cook until chutney is of desired consistency. Makes about 1 quart.

Stuffed Calamari
with Apple Banana & Cooked on the Hibachi

Serves 4

When grilling unskewered shellfish like shrimp and calamari, it's good to use a fine-meshed, well-oiled fish grate. It makes handling the smaller foods much easier. It lets the smoky flavor permeate the meat without allowing the fish to fall through the grill.

One day, a neighbor brought over a handful of really tasty apple bananas from his yard. They were small and tart and really 'ono, I got some calamari from some fishermen In Kailua-Kona, and decided to stuff the calamari with the bananas. It turned out GREAT! Try it.

1 pound fresh calamari
1 tablespoon fresh garlic, minced
1 tablespoon fresh ginger, minced
1/2 tablespoon cracked peppercorn
1/2 teaspoon fresh basil, chopped
3/4 cup Mirin (Japanese sweet
  rice wine)

2 tablespoons Aloha shoyu
2 tablespoons macadamia nut oil
1 teaspoon granulated sugar
1 tablespoon fresh cilantro, minced
12 ripe apple bananas, split in half
Tropical Fruit Salsa
  (see recipe below)

Clean calamari. In a large mixing bowl, blend all of the ingredients together, and pour over calamari. Let marinate for 1 hour. Stuff calamari lengthwise with apple bananas, then lightly score sides to add elasticity during cooking. (Be careful not to pierce through the calamari skin.) Place on the hibachi to cook for about 3 minutes on each side. Serve with Tropical Fruit Salsa.

Tropical Fruit Salsa:

1/2 cup white wine vinegar
3 tablespoons granulated sugar
1/4 teaspoon ground cumin
1/2 cup fresh cilantro, chopped
1 tablespoon fresh ginger, minced
1/2 cup mango, chopped
1/2 cup pineapple, chopped
1/2 cup papaya, chopped
1 red bell pepper, chopped
2 Hawaiian chili peppers, minced

Blend vinegar, sugar, cumin, cilantro, and ginger until sugar dissolves. Then fold into fruit, and set aside.

Tequila-Grilled Shrimp

Serves 4

This is a real "tropical-looking" dish. Years ago, I watched a Mexican fisherman on the Baja peninsula marinate his catch in tequila. I asked for a bite, and discovered a whole new flavor. I added a few of my own "local" touches. It's a mellow, "make you smile" treat.

**1 pound jumbo shrimp, peeled
and deveined**

Mix marinade ingredients in a shallow glass or plastic dish. Add shrimp, cover, and refrigerate 1 hour.

Remove shrimp from marinade; reserve marinade. Thread 6 shrimp on each of six 8-inch metal skewers. Grill over medium coals, turning once, until pink, 2 to 3 minutes on each side.

Bring marinade to boil in non-aluminum (or non-reactive) saucepan; reduce heat to low. Simmer uncovered about 5 minutes. Serve with shrimp.

Marinade:

1/4 cup corn oil
1/4 cup tequila
1/4 cup red wine vinegar
2 tablespoons fresh lime juice
1/2 teaspoon salt
1 tablespoon chili garlic sauce
1 red bell pepper, diced
1 clove fresh garlic, minced
1/3 cup onion, minced
1/4 cup fresh cilantro, minced

Combine ingredients, and set aside.

Garnish:

Papaya, Mango, Cilantro, chopped

To Broil:

Set oven control to broil. Place skewered shrimp on rack in broiler pan. Broil with tops about 4 inches from heat, turning once, until pink, 2 or 3 minutes on each side.

Lay the shrimp skewers side-by-side on a serving platter, and scatter mango and papaya chunks over the top. Sprinkle with chopped cilantro.

Marinating seafood in a flavor-enhancing liquid is a good way to preserve the moisture during cooking. Fish is quick to pick up the flavors in a marinade, so they only need 15 to 30 minutes— 1 hour at most—in their precooking bath. Shellfish require around 1 hour for the marinade to get through the shells and into the meat.

Pulehu Island Mix Grill

Serves 4

The old folks loved eating 'opihi and all small shellfish raw, doused with chili pepper water and shoyu. I decided to throw them on the grill with clams and oysters to get the smoky taste, then flavor them with chili pepper.

I put a piece of pickled Maui onion on top of grilled shellfish. Drizzle some shoyu and chili pepper water over the top, then slide it down and chew. It's real easy to make, and an art to eat. Oh yeah! Broke da mouth!

8 pieces large 'opihi
8 pieces large clams
8 pieces large oysters

Chili Pepper Water
  (see recipe below)
Aloha shoyu
pickled Maui (sweet) onion

Real simple! Get your charcoal grill nice and hot, then lay your 'opihi, clams, and oysters on top of the grill for about 3 to 4 minutes. Cook until shellfish pop open. Grill for 2 minutes more, put shellfish on a plate, then splash with your favorite sauces.

Serve with Chili Pepper Water, shoyu, and pickled Maui onions.

Chili Pepper Water:

2 Hawaiian chili peppers, chopped
1 cup water
1/4 cup vinegar
1 teaspoon Hawaiian salt
1/4 teaspoon fresh garlic, crushed

Combine all ingredients in small saucepan, and cook for 15 minutes. Blend, then cool.

Chef Sam Choy's hibachi; chili pepper water bottle provided by Jennifer Pontz of Tropical Art Glass, Holualoa, Big Island.

SEVEN

SIDES & STIR-FRY

Night Diving

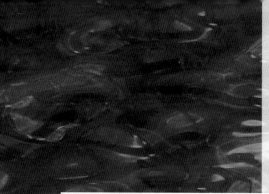

BAKER-VAN DYKE COLLECTION

The spookiest fishing is going out on no moon nights, into the ink-black water with nothing but a spear and a waterproof flashlight. All you can see is what that thin beam of light shows you.

I've watched huge white eels six feet long swimming through the darkness, and they don't even notice my light. I've floated over giant manta rays gliding through my beams like I don't know what, dark ghosts with huge wings. So spooky. I've looked into lobster caves crusted with shells and antennas, and seen uhu asleep encased in their balloons. I've run my fingers over pockets of phosphorescence and seen the tiny little blue-green lights shimmer and tumble at my touch.

The ocean at night is so different from the day, like going to another planet. Some fish—the night swimmers—are attracted to the flashlight and come close to check it out. Other fish are sleeping, tucked in under shelves in the reef. It almost seems too easy to surprise them in this way and spear them. But, really, just being there at all for the fisherman is hard, because it's so disorienting in the dark. You feel as vulnerable as the fish. You imagine all sorts of shadowy monsters creeping toward you.

And it's cold. I've never lasted more than an hour or so night diving. And most of my friends won't stay out long either. It's pretty weird.

But it's also beautiful. I've come up in the middle of nowhere—just a few fuzzy lights along the shore, and the night sky filled with stars—turned off my light, and watched the arc of the Milky Way and the millions of other stars drift in and out of clouds. And then I've swum home with my stringer loaded with fish, bound for a warm kitchen and a hot stove.

Black Goma Asparagus
with Bay Scallops

Serves 4

This dish cooks up so fast. In no time you'll be sitting at the table enjoying a delicious little feast. It's quick, it's easy, it's classic stir-fry. Cooking in a flash. Perfect for those busy days. Serve over hot rice, of course.

2 tablespoons light vegetable oil
1 pound asparagus,
   sliced into 1-inch pieces
1 pound bay scallops
1 tablespoon fresh ginger, minced
1 tablespoon fresh garlic, minced

1/4 cup chicken broth
1 tablespoon Aloha shoyu
1/2 teaspoon granulated sugar
1/2 teaspoon salt
1 tablespoon black goma
   (black sesame seeds)

Scallops are very good swimmers, moving swiftly through the water by rapidly opening and closing their valves. When the large adductor muscle closes the valves, the water between them is forced through openings near the hinge. This action jets the scallop along the ocean bottom in a zigzag fashion.

Heat vegetable oil in a wok. Add asparagus, scallops, ginger, and garlic. Cook about 1 minute. Add chicken broth, shoyu, sugar, salt, and sesame seeds, and cook another minute. Remove from wok, and serve.

Choy Sum
with "'Ono-licious" Sauce

Serves 4

Cabbage, an Oriental vegetable staple, is prepared raw, steamed, blanched, wilted, boiled, or baked. There are different varieties found all over Asia, from choy sum, much like Western kale or spinach, to bok choy, the Chinese mustard cabbage. Most of these cabbages are interchangeable, and substitution is encouraged.

For a taste of the Orient, try this unusual and healthful dish. You can substitute other greens if you like, but ung choy and choy sum are usually available in your local market, and the sauce was created with these vegetables in mind.

1 teaspoon cooking oil
1 bunch ung choy (Chinese
   hollow-stemmed cabbage)
1 bunch choy sum (Chinese
   leafy green vegetable,
   like spinach or kale)

"'Ono-licious" Sauce
   (see recipe below)
salt and pepper to taste

Fill a pot half full of water. Bring to a fast boil. Add 1 teaspoon of oil to boiling water. Add vegetables, season with salt and pepper, and cook for 1 minute or until just wilted. Drain. Rinse under cold running water. Drain. Squeeze to remove excess water. Cut into 2-inch lengths. Arrange on platter, and pour on the sauce.

"'Ono-licious" Sauce:

1 tablespoon Aloha shoyu
2 tablespoons Mirin (Japanese
   sweet rice wine)
1 teaspoon sesame oil
1 teaspoon oyster sauce
1 teaspoon granulated sugar

Mix well.

Honoka'a-Style Bread Stuffing

Serves 8–10

I developed this recipe in honor of one of my friends of Portuguese descent.
He said that his mom used to make an "unreal" stuffing using sausage and sweet
bread. But he didn't have any sisters, and, when his mom passed away, the recipe
was gone with her. When he tried it, he said, "It's not exactly the same as
Mama's, but it's REAL close."

1/2 cup bacon, chopped
1 whole Portuguese sausage
  (preferably Uncle Louie),
    1/2-inch diced
1/2 cup butter
2 cups round onion, diced
2 cups celery, diced
1 bell pepper, diced

2 tablespoons poultry seasoning,
  or to taste
6 cups chicken broth
6 cups sweet bread crumbs
1 cup sweet potato,
  cooked and cubed
salt and pepper to taste

Sauté bacon for about 1 minute. Add Portuguese sausage, and sauté for another
1-1/2 minutes. Remove excess oil from pan. Add 4 tablespoons butter, onions,
celery, and bell pepper. Sauté for about 5 minutes or until onions are translucent.
Add poultry seasoning, and sauté for 1 minute. Add chicken broth, and simmer
for 8 minutes. Remove from heat, and add sweet bread crumbs and sweet potatoes.
Salt and pepper to taste.

The Portuguese cowboys (paniolo) helped introduce some of the most beloved food in our mixed Island culture. Who can resist the spicy aroma of Portuguese sausages frying on the stove, or the taste of soft, yellow sweet bread?

Baked Coconut Taro

Serves 4

In Hawai'i, taro has been the staple from earliest times to the present, and its culture developed to include more than 300 types. The entire plant is eaten, from its starchy root (often mashed into poi) to its heart-shaped leaves (known as lu'au).

This side dish combines the most basic of Polynesian flavors, coconut and taro, and goes well with any seafood dish. It's also one of the easiest ways to add authentic Island-style starch to your meal.

1 pound fresh taro root, blanched and cubed
1/4 cup butter

1/4 cup coconut syrup
salt and white pepper to taste

Combine taro, butter, coconut syrup, salt, and pepper in a covered casserole dish, and bake in 350° oven for 35 minutes.

To serve, garnish with toasted coconut and chopped roasted macadamia nuts.

Garnish:

coconut flakes, toasted
macadamia nuts, roasted and chopped

GOSSAMER BAY.
VINEYARDS

CALIFORNIA
CHARDONNAY
1995

ALC. 13% BY VOL.

Bronze poi pounder done by Stephen Kofsky of Kofsky Fine Arts, Kailua-Kona, Big Island; bowls lent by Liberty House—Ala Moana; lei made by Norman "Buzzy" Histo of Kalikokalehua Hula Studio, Kamuela, Big Island; koa wood sashimi platform lent by Liberty House—Kailua-Kona, Big Island.

Kahuku Corn Smashed Potatoes

Serves 6–8

Kahuku, once a plantation town near the northern tip of O'ahu, struggled after the sugar mill closed in the 1970s. Some plantation workers' families leased land from the Campbell Estate that owned the land, and started farms in fields once used to raise sweet sugar cane. Today, they harvest and sell some of the sweetest corn and juiciest watermelons in the world.

There really isn't anything as sweet as eating Kahuku corn on a warm summer evening. This recipe, featuring a mixture of corn and potatoes, is a kua'aina treat, even if you live in the big city.

3 pounds potatoes, peeled and cubed into 1-inch pieces
1-1/2 teaspoons salt
1/2 cup sweet butter
1 large round onion, diced
1/2 teaspoon ground cumin

5 cloves fresh garlic, peeled and minced
2-1/4 cups fresh corn kernels
3/4 cup milk
1-1/2 teaspoons fresh cilantro, finely chopped
salt and pepper to taste

Place potatoes in a pot. Cover with water, and salt. Bring water to a boil, and cook until tender.

Meanwhile, heat butter in a small skillet, and sauté onions, cumin, and garlic until tender; about 3 to 4 minutes. Add corn, and cook for 2 minutes more. Add milk, and simmer for 1 to 2 minutes. Add cilantro, and salt and pepper to taste.

Remove potatoes from heat, and drain. Mash the potatoes, and add corn mixture. Serve hot.

Kona Flaming Wok Clams in Shells

Serves 4–6

This is already a pretty spicy recipe, but you can punch it up by adding one or two hot chili peppers to the mix. That's a great addition, give it a try. To make this dish correctly, it must be cooked in one of my "Kona Flaming Woks." Just kidding.

24 clams	2 tablespoons Aloha shoyu
4 tablespoons vegetable oil	1 tablespoon brown sugar
3 cloves fresh garlic, minced	1/2 teaspoon salt
1 tablespoon fresh ginger, minced	1 Hawaiian chili pepper,
1/2 cup chicken stock	minced (optional)
1 Maui (sweet) onion, julienned	

Wash clams. Heat wok, and add oil. Let oil get smoky without having a flame. Add clams, garlic, ginger, and chicken stock to wok all together. Cover, and let cook for 2 to 3 minutes. Add remaining ingredients. Let cook for 5 to 8 minutes, and garnish with green onions and cilantro.

Garnish:

green onions
fresh cilantro

> *Woks are used all over Asia. They are made from cast iron, carbon steel, aluminum, stainless steel, or copper. I've developed an entire line of woks that come in different sizes to accommodate handgrip, arm strength, and cooking preference.*

Hibachi Mixed Vegetables

Serves 4

These marinated vegetables are wonderful just off the grill. Sometimes, they fall through the spaces during cooking. I usually use a grid or grilling mesh when barbecuing small pieces of food like shellfish or vegetables. It's just much easier—less frustrating.

1 piece zucchini, sliced oval
1 piece yellow squash, sliced oval
1 piece red bell pepper, cut
  into wedges
6 pieces shiitake mushrooms
1 teaspoon fresh garlic, chopped
1/4 teaspoon black pepper
1/4 teaspoon chili sauce

1 teaspoon cilantro, chopped
1 teaspoon thyme leaves, chopped
1 tablespoon white wine
1 tablespoon salad oil
1 tablespoon sesame oil
1/4 teaspoon Aloha shoyu
1/4 teaspoon oyster sauce

Mix all ingredients together. Let marinate for 1/2 hour. Cook over charcoal broiler or hibachi.

Carrots and Cranberries

Serves 4

The bright colors make this a particularly attractive dish, and a perfect selection for any holiday. Cranberries, carrots, an apple, and brown sugar blend to complement any seafood entrée.

Cranberries are a sour-tasting red berry that grows on creeping shrubs. It's possible to substitute gooseberry, like the Hawaiian poha berries, in this recipe to make it a little more exotic.

1 cup fresh cranberries
1 apple
4 cups carrots, grated
1 tablespoon brown sugar

1/2 teaspoon salt
1/2 cup apple cider
2 tablespoons butter

Preheat oven to 350°.

Wash cranberries.

Grate the apple, and mix with cranberries, carrots, brown sugar, salt, and apple cider.

Place ingredients in a buttered casserole, and dot with butter.

Cover, and bake for 40 minutes. Stir once during the baking.

Shiitake Mushroom Rice
with Shredded Ono Stir-Fry and Fresh Spinach

Serves 4

Hawai'i's troll-caught ono are marketed at fish auctions in Honolulu and Hilo. But the long-line ono catch is primarily sold through the Honolulu auction. Sometimes the fishermen sell their catch directly to restaurants. Because of seasonal conditions, it's not possible for restaurants to get fresh ono year around, so chefs are quick to snap up this tasty fish when it's available.

A wonderful combination of protein, starch, and green vegetables, this mouth-watering recipe pulls ingredients from several Pacific cultures into one unforgettable Island-style potpourri of flavors.

1 tablespoon light olive oil
1 medium onion, julienned
1 cup fresh shiitake mushrooms, sliced
2 teaspoons fresh garlic, minced
1 tablespoon fresh ginger, minced

3 ono (wahoo) fillets, cut diagonally in thin strips
1/2 cup chicken broth
3 tablespoons oyster sauce
1 pound fresh spinach, chopped
salt and pepper to taste
6 cups Basmati rice, cooked

In a wok, heat oil. Stir-fry onion, shiitake mushrooms, garlic, and ginger for 1 minute. Add ono, and cook for 30 seconds, stirring constantly. Add chicken broth and oyster sauce; cook for 1 minute.

Add spinach, and salt and pepper to taste. Cook until spinach is wilted.

Serve over hot Basmati rice.

Garnish

straw mushrooms

Wok provided by Liberty House; flowers donated by Norman "Buzzy" Histo of Kalikokalehua Hula Studio, Kamuela, Big Island.

Paniolo Potato Hash

Serves 4

Pipi kaula is beef, salted and dried in the sun, then broiled before eating. The literal translation of this Hawaiian word is "rope beef." This was a saddlebag staple for the paniolo (cowboys) as they rode the sloped pastures of Upcountry Maui and the Kohala area of the Big Island.

This recipe goes well with the Ginger Pesto-Crusted 'Opakapaka and the Sautéed Mahimahi with Warm Corn Sauce. Dress up the patties by sprinkling chopped green onion over them.

2 tablespoons butter
1 cup pipi kaula (pepper-cured beef), diced
1 medium onion, diced small
1-1/2 teaspoons fresh garlic, minced

4 cups mashed potatoes, cooked
1 large whole egg
1/2 cup all-purpose flour
4 tablespoons oil, for frying
salt and pepper to taste

Heat butter, and sauté pipi kaula for 1 minute. Add onions and garlic, and sauté for 2 to 3 minutes. Add to hot mashed potatoes, and mix in 1 raw egg to bind. Add salt and pepper to taste.

Refrigerate for at least an hour, or overnight, and then shape mixture into 8 patties. Coat lightly with flour. Fry in oil on both sides (3-1/2 minutes on each side) at medium heat until crisp on the outside. Serve hot.

Sam Choy's Lop Cheong Fried Rice

Serves 4

The fun thing about making fried rice is the kind of layering effect of its creation. You start out small and just add and add more ingredients, each one contributing its flavors, until you have built a pan full of perfect fried rice.

1 tablespoon vegetable oil
6 pieces lop cheong (Chinese pork sausage), sliced thin diagonally
1 cup round onion, diced small
1/2 cup celery, minced
1/2 cup carrots, grated
1-1/2 teaspoons fresh garlic, minced
1-1/2 teaspoons fresh ginger, minced

6 cups rice, cooked
3 tablespoons oyster sauce
1 tablespoon Aloha shoyu
salt and pepper to taste
1/2 green onion, for garnish
1/2 cup red and white kamaboko (fish cakes), diced small, for garnish

Pour the oil in a non-stick wok pan, and sauté the lop cheong for 2 minutes on medium-high heat. Drain excess oil. Sauté onion, celery, carrots, garlic, and ginger for 2 to 3 minutes over medium-high heat. Add cooked rice, and sauté for about 3 minutes. Add oyster sauce, shoyu, and salt and pepper to taste, and sauté until rice mixture dries. Garnish with green onions and kamaboko. Serve hot with your favorite seafood entrée.

Garnish:

1/2 cup green onion
1/2 cup red and white kamaboko (fish cake), diced small

> Fried rice—cooked rice stir-fried with bits of meat and vegetables and flavored with shoyu—is a popular snack in China; you can serve it as a speedy and nutritious one-dish meal. For successful fried rice, you must start with cold cooked rice. If it isn't cold to begin with, the grains won't stay separate, and you'll end up with a sticky mix of rice and ingredients.

Steve's Kona Ogo Coleslaw

Serves 4

Steven A. Katase, owner/operator of the Royal Hawaiian Sea Farms in Kona, gave
me this delightful recipe. We get most of our ogo from Steve's pools. Only an
aquaculture expert like Steve could come up with such an original dish for ogo.

2 cups thick ogo, coarsely chopped
1/4 cup won bok (Chinese cabbage),
  shredded
1/4 cup carrots, shredded
1/4 cup red bell pepper, sliced thin
1/4 cup daikon (white radish),
  shredded
1 tablespoon Aloha shoyu
1 cup rice vinegar

2 tablespoons granulated sugar
1 teaspoon chili pepper flakes
2 tablespoons fresh cilantro,
  chopped
1 tablespoon goma
  (black sesame seeds)
1 tablespoon fresh ginger slivers
1 tablespoon light olive oil

*Daikon, a white-fleshed root much
like the Western white radishes,
may grow as long as 14 inches
and weigh a hefty 4 to 5 pounds.
Japanese cooks simmer daikon
in soups, preserve it in pungent
pickles, and serve it raw (finely
shredded, it's the classic garnish
for sushi and sashimi). Western
white radishes are an acceptable
substitute for raw daikon; use
small turnips in place of daikon
that's to be simmered.*

Mix all ingredients together, and prepare yourself for a new sensation!

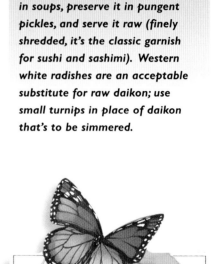

Etched glass bowl made by Gary Wagner of
Plaza Pacific Design, Kamuela, Big Island;
etched glass balls made by Jennifer Pontz of Tropical
Art Glass, Holualoa, Big Island.

Stir-Fried Chili-Garlic Shrimp

Serves 4

Shrimp cook up very quickly, and pick up other flavors easily. For this reason, shrimp has become one of the most popular shellfishes in seaside communities around the world. They are deep-fried, stir fried, sautéed, pan fried, boiled, broiled, or barbecued. Whatever the cooking method, shrimp has a way of turning out just perfect.

The most interesting thing about stir-frying dishes is that it takes more time to cut, dice, and prepare the ingredients than it does to cook them. This is a straightforward shrimp dish. There's nothing to cut, just measure your ingredients, heat the wok, and go. Amazingly simple, but amazingly good.

1 tablespoon salad oil
1 tablespoon fresh garlic, minced
24 large shrimp (16-20 pieces
   per pound), shelled and deveined
1 tablespoon sambal oelek (chili paste)
1-1/2 tablespoons brown sugar

1/2 cup ketchup
1-1/2 tablespoons cider vinegar
2 tablespoons sherry wine
2 tablespoons Aloha shoyu
salt and pepper to taste

Garnish:

2 cups bean sprouts
4 cilantro sprigs
4 lemon wedges

Heat wok, add oil. Sauté garlic. Add shrimp, and stir-fry over high heat for 1 minute. Add remaining ingredients, and stir for 1-1/2 minutes. Serve on a bed of fresh bean sprouts, and garnish with chopped cilantro and lemon wedges.

Waipi'o Ho'i'o Kim Chee

In Korea, kim chee is eaten at every meal. Traditionally, it is made in autumn, in batches large enough to last a family through the following winter and spring. The spicy, pickled cabbage mixture is packed in large crocks, then allowed to ferment.

Kim Chee and fish, the perfect match. Serve it as a condiment with a nice grilled fish. It's hot and spicy. Or, Island-style, as a chaser or pupu. Serve with hibachi food, whatevah.

2 cups ho'i'o ferns, blanched,
   and cut into 2-inch lengths
1 cup cucumber, seeds removed,
   and cut into 2-inch long spears
1/2 cup green onion, chopped
1-2 fresh garlic cloves, minced

1 teaspoon ginger, minced
2 tablespoons granulated sugar
1 tablespoon sambal oelek (chili paste)
1 tablespoon fish sauce
salt to taste

Garnish:

1 tablespoon black goma
   (black sesame seeds)

Mix ingredients together, and marinate for at least 1 hour before serving. Garnish with black goma before serving.

Wok Lobster
with Fresh Kona Oyster Mushrooms

Serves 4

The flavors and textures in this dish are surprising. It's a different and slightly decadent way to cook up lobster. I am such a fan of lobster, that having bite-size pieces of the tender white meat in any dish is a taste treat.

1 tablespoon cornstarch
2 tablespoons Aloha shoyu
1 tablespoon sherry
1 pound fresh lobster meat,
 cut into 1-inch cubes
1 pound fresh oyster mushrooms
 or mushrooms of your choice—
 try shiitake mushrooms—yummy!

1 cup green onion, cut in
 1-inch pieces
2 to 3 tablespoons vegetable oil
1 cup chicken stock
salt and white pepper to taste

In a large mixing bowl, make a cornstarch paste using the shoyu and sherry, and mix in the lobster meat.

Slice the fresh oyster mushrooms into large chunks, and set aside.

Cut green onion stalks in 1-inch sections. Heat your Kona Flaming Wok with 2 to 3 tablespoons of oil, then add lobster mixture. Cook for 2 to 3 minutes. Add chicken stock, mushrooms, and green onions. Salt and pepper to taste. Let simmer for 2 to 3 minutes more; keep stirring to blend all flavors. Serve at once.

When you stir-fry, remember that the cooking times in recipes are just suggestions! Much depends on the intensity of the heat source you use, and on the thickness of food slices. Times can vary greatly. Prepare everything before you begin stir-frying—know the recipe's overall cooking sequence, everything prepared before you begin (once the wok is hot, there's no time for slicing and dicing), and use our cooking times as a guide.

Stir-Fried Dungeness Crab
and Black Beans

Serves 2

The fermentation process in making shoyu involves letting soybeans sit until they turn black. Cooks discovered that these black soybeans really enhance the flavor of seafood. Remember, be careful to use black beans sparingly, because they're quite salty, and their strong flavor might overwhelm the seafood.

Black beans are magic with fresh seafood, and more chefs are catching on to its wild fermented flavor and saltiness. This recipe is a particular favorite of mine.

1 whole Dungeness crab
2 tablespoons vegetable oil
2 tablespoons fermented
   black bean paste
1 cup chicken stock
1 tablespoon Aloha shoyu
1 tablespoon oyster sauce

1 teaspoon sesame oil
1/4 teaspoon chili flakes
1 tablespoon granulated sugar
1-1/2 tablespoons cornstarch and
   3 tablespoons water for thickening
2 cups stir-fried vegetables

Rinse crab, remove the top shell. Separate the claws from the body, discarding head and innards. Crack the claws, and quarter the body. Heat oil, add crab and black bean paste. Stir-fry for 2 minutes. Add chicken stock, shoyu, oyster sauce, sesame oil, chili flakes, and sugar. Cook for 5 minutes, and thicken with cornstarch and water. Serve with cooked stir-fry vegetables.

Plate etched by Jennifer Pontz of Tropical Art Glass, Holualoa, Big Island; fabric designed by Hina Lei Creations, Kamuela, Big Island; flower vase by Kyle Ino of Kyle Ino Designs, Kane'ohe, O'ahu; flowers donated by Marie McDonald.

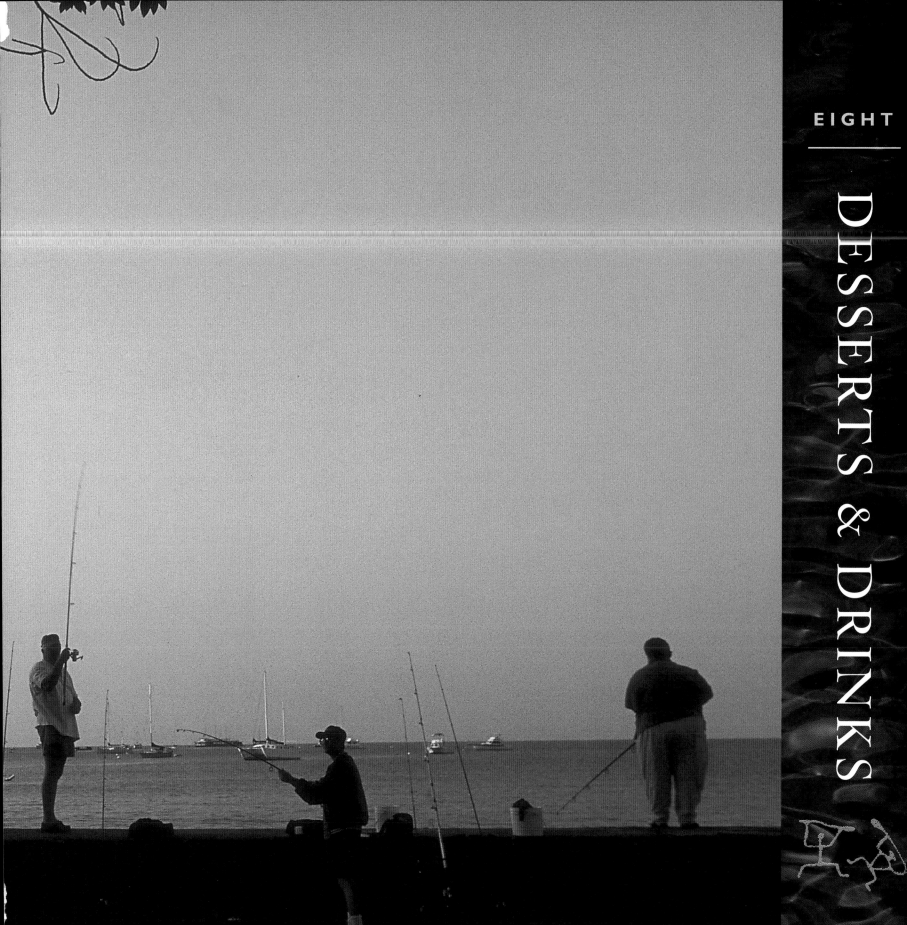

DESSERTS & DRINKS

Squidding

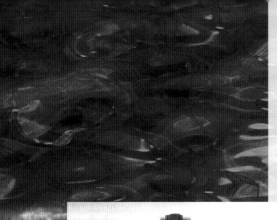

I used to go out in the old days in Lā'ie Bay and spend hours squidding. It takes a lot of patience to search the reefs and find the squid. They're everywhere but so hard to spot because of their ability to camouflage themselves.

When locals say "squid" we mean octopus, and going squidding means hunting for octopus. Sure, everyone knows the difference between real squid—the cephalopod mollusk that is free-swimming and has an elongated body and ten legs—and the octopus, which is a reef crawler that has a rounded, saclike body, distinct head, and eight tentacles with suckers on them. We eat octopus and call it squid.

If you have a good "squid eye" you can spot the octopus hiding in the reef. Squidders usually go out at low tide with a squid box—a wooden square with a glass bottom—and peer through it at the reef. Sometimes (and I used to do this in the old days) they'll chew coconut and spit the oil on the water. Like magic the ripples smooth, the water clears, and you can see right to the bottom. I used to chew what we call "bolo-head coconut," which is dry inside: more oil.

When you catch an octopus, you bite the eye then turn the ala-ala bag (its head and body) inside out to kill it right away. It's the most humane way.

Most folks hang squid on lines in the sun and seabreeze to dry the meat. This makes them more tasty. Then they pound the meat with wooden mallets to soften it up for cooking or eating raw.

Call it "reef demon" or octopus or whatever, for unusual texture and exotic flavor, there's nothing in the world like good squid.

Apple Cobbler

Serves 8

My apple cobbler is topped with a sweet, crunchy streusel layer that is browned to a heavy crust. Serve it hot with vanilla ice cream. I add slivered almonds sometimes, just for an added crunch.

Cinnamon Mixture:

8 cups Granny Smith apple slices
1-1/2 cups brown sugar
1 cup bread flour
1 tablespoon ground cinnamon

Peel and core apples. Slice into 16ths. Mix all ingredients together. Sprinkle over apple slices. Mix well, and place into glass custard cups. Top heavily with streusel.

Streusel:

1-1/2 cups butter
1-1/2 cups granulated sugar
3 cups bread flour

Mix butter and sugar till partially creamy. Add flour slowly. Mix until crumbly. Do not overmix. Top apple mixture heavily with streusel. Bake at 350° for 45–50 minutes, until golden brown.

Garnish:

vanilla ice cream
almonds, slivered

Cobbler, a very old dessert, is a deep-dish pie (usually with fruit) topped with a thick crust. The same recipe can be made using any other seasonal fruit such as peaches, blackberries, or plums. The origin of this type of dessert lies somewhere in the farmlands of rural Europe.

Chocolate, Chocolate-Chip Cheesecake

Serves 12

I periodically serve this cheesecake in my restaurants. It's very rich and after eating a meal at a Sam Choy's, many of my patrons decide to share this dessert. One woman shared one with her husband recently, then bought another slice to take home and eat later.

There's just no denying the high fat content in any cheesecake. The use of the basic ingredients—cream cheese, sugar, and eggs—makes this one of the most calorically dense desserts known to man. But all of that aside, it's still one of the most requested treats in the United States.

Oreo Cookie Crust:

2 cups Oreo cookies, centers removed, and chocolate cookies crushed

1/2 cup granulated sugar
1/2 cup butter, melted

Mix all ingredients together. Grease a 10-inch springform pan. Press crust firmly into bottom of pan. Bake for 5 minutes at 350°.

Chocolate Cheesecake:

2 pounds cream cheese, at room temperature
1-1/2 cups granulated sugar
1/3 cup cocoa, unsweetened powder
6 eggs
1-1/2 cups chocolate chips

Cream the cream cheese, sugar, and cocoa together. Add eggs. Add chocolate chips. Pour over Oreo Cookie Crust. Bake at 300° for 1-1/2 hours to 2 hours, until outer edge of the cake is set. Chill for at least 4 hours. Remove from pan.

Ganaché:

1 cup heavy cream
2 cups chocolate chips

Bring heavy cream to boil. Pour cream over chocolate chips, and stir until smooth. Place chilled cheesecake on a cooling rack. Place cooling rack on a cooking sheet. Pour warm ganaché over cheesecake to glaze. Then decorate by pressing chocolate chips on edges of cake. Chill for 1/2 hour, then cut into 12 slices.

Garnish:

chocolate chips

Coconut Bread Pudding

Serves 8

Coconut Bread Pudding is a staple dessert at my *Breakfast, Lunch and Crab* Restaurant in Iwilei. We top it with a scoop of ice cream (sometimes vanilla, sometimes coconut). If you want to test this dessert out before you make it, come on down.

3 eggs
3/4 cup granulated sugar
4 cups milk
6 tablespoons coconut milk

8 cups diced bread—
   about 1/2-inch cubes
1/2 cup toasted macadamia nuts,
   chopped
1/2 cup toasted coconut flakes

Whisk eggs and sugar together. Add milk and coconut milk, and mix thoroughly.

Layer bread, macadamia nuts, and coconut flakes in a 9-inch x 13-inch pan. Pour custard mixture evenly over top, and let custard soak into bread. Bake at 325° for 45 minutes to 1 hour, until it tests clean when a toothpick is inserted.

When serving, drizzle about 2 tablespoons of coconut syrup over each portion. Top with a swirl of whipped cream. Sprinkle with diced pineapple, macadamia nuts, and coconut flakes.

Garnish: (per serving)

2 tablespoons coconut syrup
toasted macadamia nuts, chopped
toasted coconut flakes
pineapple, diced
whipped cream

Bread pudding originated in bakeries as a way to use up day-old goods. Adding a custard-style mixture of eggs, sugar, and milk to diced bread cubes, moistened the bread into a hearty, dense pudding. Frontier families enjoyed this delicious dessert whenever there were surplus loaves.

Crème Brûlée

Serves 4

This is not a French dessert dish. Originally, it appeared in a seventeenth century English cookbook under the title "burnt cream." It was a favorite confection at the Corpus Christi College at Cambridge University, where it picked up the more flamboyant French name "Crème Brûlée." Many different recipes for this dish have come down through the years. This is one I developed for my restaurants.

1/2 cup milk	6 egg yolks
2 cups heavy cream	1 teaspoon vanilla extract
1/2 cup brown sugar	4 tablespoons superfine sugar

Preheat oven to 350°. Set up brûlée dishes on sheet pans. Scald milk, half of the cream, and half of the brown sugar. Beat egg yolks in a mixing bowl. Add the remaining brown sugar and the vanilla extract to the egg yolks, and beat until smooth. Add the remaining cream to the egg yolk mixture. Gradually stir the hot cream mixture into the yolk mixture. Strain the Crème Brûlée through a strainer, and skim off the foam.

Pour Crème Brûlée mixture into 4 brûlée dishes, leaving about 1/8-inch at the top (about 5 ounces per dish). Put a sheet pan in the oven, and fill it with water to make a hot water bath. Bake at 300° for 35 to 50 minutes. Rotate the sheet pan to provide for even baking and to avoid overcooking the ones in the hottest parts of the oven. Bake just until the custard sets. Test to see if dessert is done by slightly tilting the brûlée dishes; if there is a bulge in the Crème Brûlée or if it is soupy in the center, it needs to cook some more. When finished cooking, remove from the oven and the hot water bath. Let the Crème Brûlée sit at room temperature for 30 minutes. Refrigerate custard for several hours to overnight.

Just before serving:

Preheat the broiler until it is very hot. Sprinkle 1 tablespoon of superfine sugar over each custard. Place the custards approximately 3 inches from the broiler. Broil until the sugar is caramelized. Allow the sugar to harden for a couple of minutes, then serve.

Painted wooden fish provided by Nancy James, Host Marriott Corp., Polynesian Cultural Center, La'ie, O'ahu; bowl provided by Liberty House—Ala Moana, Honolulu, O'ahu; plate provided by Kevin P. Nutt, West Hawaii Foodworks, Kamuela, Big Island; fabric by Jan of Hina Lei Creations, Kamuela, Big Island.

Macadamia Nut Cream Pie

Serves 8

Living in the Kona district on the Big Island gives me great opportunities to create dishes using premium macadamia nuts. I pick the best of the crop, and use them in my recipes and restaurants.

3 egg yolks
3 cups milk
3/4 cup granulated sugar
1/3 cup cornstarch
1/4 teaspoon salt

2 tablespoons butter
1-1/2 teaspoons vanilla extract
1 cup macadamia nuts,
 roasted and chopped
1 9-inch baked pie shell

Combine egg yolks, milk, sugar, cornstarch, salt, and butter. Bring to a boil over medium heat, stirring constantly. Boil for 1 minute, and remove from heat. Stir in vanilla and macadamia nuts. Pour into pie shell, and chill covered with plastic wrap.

Garnish: (per serving)

2 tablespoons whipped cream
1 tablespoon macadamia nuts,
 coarsely chopped

Sam Choy's Pineapple Cheesecake
with Macadamia Nut Crust

175

Serves 8

We are currently serving this very popular pineapple cheesecake at my Diamond Head restaurant. The candy-nut crust sets off the creamy cheese filling. Serve each piece on a bed of *Cream Anglaise*, with colorful fresh fruits, i.e. strawberries, raspberries, blackberries, kiwi. Enjoy!

On the mainland, every recipe that's labeled "Hawaiian" includes some form of pineapple—pineapple juice, crushed pineapple, pineapple chunks, pineapple slices. This is because of the Oriental sweet/sour flavor that's so popular in Island cuisine.

Crust:

1 cup macadamia nuts
1/2 cup granulated sugar
3 tablespoons sweet butter, melted

Chop the macadamia nuts in a food processor to a coarse-meal consistency, but not so fine that the oil from the nuts makes them sticky. Combine the sugar with the nuts. Stream in the butter while mixing.

Filling:

3-1/2 8-ounce packages of
  cream cheese
1-1/4 cups granulated sugar
pinch of orange zest (optional)
pinch of lemon zest (optional)
1/4 cup heavy cream
1-1/2 cups sour cream
4 large eggs
1 pineapple, diced small

Soften the cream cheese, sugar, and zest together in a power mixer or food processor. Add the cream, sour cream, and eggs one ingredient at a time, mixing well, and scraping the bowl down before adding the next ingredient.

Assembly and Baking:

Preheat oven to 350°. Grease the cake pan and lay a circle of parchment or waxed paper on the bottom. Pack the crust in the bottom of the pan and bake for 5 to 10 minutes until very lightly brown. In a towel, squeeze some of the juice out of the pineapple. Pour half the batter filling on top of the pre-baked crust. Stir the pineapple into the rest of the batter. Pour the rest of the batter into the cake pan, and smooth the top. Now it's time to make the caramel swirl in the cake. Using a squeeze bottle, take 1/2 cup of the caramel sauce and swirl on top of the cake batter. To achieve more of a swirl, take the tip of the knife and gently swirl the caramel. Bake in a water bath for 1 hour and 15 minutes to 1-1/2 hours. Test with a skewer or paring knife to see when the cake is done. Let cool, and then chill for at least 3 hours.

Caramel Sauce:

2-1/2 cups granulated sugar
1 cup water
1 tablespoon lemon juice
3 cups cream

Make caramel from sugar, water, and lemon juice, and remove from heat. Scald the cream. Slowly add cream to the caramel. Bring back to boil just enough to melt all the sugar.

THE CHOY OF SEAFOOD | DESSERTS & DRINKS

Haupia Profiteroles

Serves 4

Profiteroles are small, puffed pastry shells that are usually filled with a custard pudding, and dusted with powdered sugar. Mine have a haupia filling with a sprinkling of sweetened coconut flakes. I must admit, it's a little rich, so use it as a special dish for special occasions.

1 cup butter
2 cups bread flour
7 eggs
Haupia Filling (see recipe below)

Boil the water and butter, then turn heat off. Add bread flour, stir until combined. Return to medium heat, and cook until the batter forms a ball, about 3 minutes. Place in mixer on #2 speed, and mix until there is no more steam and the bowl is cool on the outside. Add the eggs slowly, one at a time. Mix thoroughly.

Using a pastry bag with a plain medium-size tip, pipe the batter in 1-1/2-inch diameter balls onto sheet pans lined with parchment paper. Bake at 400° for 15 minutes. Then lower heat to 325° and bake for 40 minutes. DO NOT OPEN THE OVEN WHILE PROFITEROLES ARE BAKING OR THEY WILL COLLAPSE!

Cool. When ready to serve, cut profiteroles in half, and fill with haupia filling.

Haupia Filling:

4 cups water
2 ounces or 1/4 can coconut milk
1-1/4 cups granulated sugar
1/2 cup butter
1/2 cup cornstarch
2 cups water

Bring the water, coconut milk, sugar, and butter to a boil. Mix together the cornstarch and water. After the coconut mixture comes to a boil, add the cornstarch mixture, and stir until thickened.

Pour into a glass bowl, and cover haupia directly with plastic wrap. Cool overnight. Use ice cream scoop to fill the profiteroles.

Garnish:

whipped cream
strawberries
sweetened coconut flakes
powdered sugar

PRESENTATION

Place 3 profiteroles on a plate. Make a rosette of whipped cream in the middle of the profiteroles and in between them on the outside. Place a profiterole in the middle of the whipped cream. Stick a quarter strawberry on each of the rosettes. Sprinkle with sweetened coconut flakes just before serving.

Plate provided by Liberty House—
Ala Moana, Honolulu, O'ahu; flowers donated by Harvey and Denise Truck, Hilo, Big Island; strawberries by Michael Prine of Strawberry Hawaii, Inc., Kamuela, Big Island.

Lemon Tart

Serves 8

There's a bit of an art to rolling out the dough for the tart crust— temperature and consistency are really important. Take the dough from the refrigerator just before you plan to roll it. It should be cold, but workable. Let it stand at room temperature to take the chill off. If it cracks, wait a minute to let it warm up a little longer. If it sticks to the rolling surface of the rolling pin, you've waited too long. Put it back in the refrigerator for a minute or so. Be sure to roll it out on a lightly floured surface.

The grains of vanilla pod are important in this recipe. They give off a little burst of vanilla flavor in the crust. In my restaurants, we use a flan pan to make this thin zesty tart, and serve it without much fanfare, just a little slice of lemon on the side.

2-1/4 cups plain flour
3/4 cup confectioner's sugar
1 cup butter, diced
zest of 1 lemon, grated
grains from 1 vanilla pod

1-1/2 eggs
1/4 cup sieved confectioner's
  sugar for dusting
butter for greasing

Pre-heat the oven to 350°. Sieve the flour and sugar, and work in the butter. Make a well in the flour mixture, and add the lemon zest and vanilla grains. Beat the eggs, and add to the well. Knead the mixture with your fingers, then wrap in cling wrap. Let rest for 30 minutes in the refrigerator.

Remove pastry dough from the refrigerator, and let rest for a moment to take the chill out. Roll out the pastry on a lightly floured surface to a size just large enough to fill the flan tin or ring to be used. Fold the dough into either a greased flan ring on a greased baking sheet, or a greased flan tin with a removable base. Gently ease the dough into the corners of the tin, ensuring a good 1/2-inch overhang. DO NOT CUT THIS OFF.

Line the flan with grease-proof paper, and fill with enough dry baking beans or lentils to ensure that the sides as well as the base are weighted. This helps give a good "finished flan" shape.

Bake in the oven for 10 minutes. After 10 minutes, remove the beans and grease-proof paper, and trim the overhang from the flan. Return the flan to the oven for 10 minutes more.

Lemon Filling:

9 eggs
1-3/4 cups Caster sugar
5 lemons (zests of 2 and juice of all 5)
1 cup double cream

Whisk the eggs with sugar and the lemon zest. Stir in the lemon juice, then fold in the cream. Remove any froth from the top of the mixture.

To Make Flan:

Reduce the oven temperature to 250°. Pour the cold lemon filling into the hot pastry (this ensures that the pastry case will be sealed and hold the filling) and bake for 30 minutes in the oven.

To Serve:

Pre-heat a very hot grill. Sieve the confectioner's sugar over the tart as soon as it comes out of the oven, and then flash it briefly under the grill to caramelize the sugar. Cut into 8 slices.

Macadamia Nut Banana Cake

Serves 4 - 6

My wife Carol is the real dessert expert in our family. She makes the best turnovers, and the best double-crusted pies in the world. I enjoy watching her bake, but she always kicks me out of the kitchen. She says baking is not like cooking—you can't just throw in a little of this and a little of that. She says it's more of a science; it has to be exact, you have to stick to the recipe. She's taught me a lot about baking.

This is one of my family's favorite recipes. In fact, it's one of our friends' favorites as well. My wife makes this Macadamia Nut Banana Cake in small pans so we can hand it out to our neighbors and friends at Christmas. We sometimes put a cream cheese frosting on it with a sprinkling of mac nuts. It's rich, and festive.

1-3/4 cups butter, softened
2 cups granulated sugar
4 cups all-purpose flour, sifted
1 tablespoon baking powder
6 eggs

1 pound raw macadamia nuts, coarsely chopped
1 pound firm apple bananas, chopped
2 tablespoons vanilla extract

Preheat oven to 250°.

Cream butter and sugar. Measure sifted flour, then sift with baking powder. Add eggs and flour, alternately, to creamed butter/sugar mixture. Add nuts, chopped bananas, and vanilla.

Pour into a large, well-greased tube pan (the kind you make angel food cake in). Before baking, place a pan of water on the oven rack below; the steam will keep the cake moist during cooking.

Bake at 250° for 2 to 3 hours. Test with toothpick to see when the cake is done.

Key Lime Pie

Serves 8

Florida is the primary supplier of key limes for North America. These yellow-green limes, grown in the Florida Keys, are known for their intense citrus bite. Local grocers carry bottled Key lime juice, and sometimes, in the summer, you'll find fresh Key limes glowing in the fruit sections.

The cool, tangy flavor of Key Lime Pie is very attractive during the hot months of summer. I always use fresh Key limes from Florida. They are the difference between a fabulous pie, and a good one.

Crust:

2 cups graham cracker crumbs
1/4 cup granulated sugar
2 tablespoons butter, melted

Mix all ingredients together. Press into greased pie pan, and bake at 325° for 10 minutes. Let cool.

Garnish:

lime rind curl
whipped cream

Filling:

14 ounces condensed milk
3 egg yolks
1/2 cup Key lime juice

Combine all ingredients.

Add filling to cooled crust, and bake at 325° for 10 to 15 minutes, until filling is set in the middle. Let pie cool. Spread 1/4 cup whipped cream evenly over top of cooled pie.

Garnish with a lime rind curl in the middle of whipped cream topping.

Kou paddle by artist J.K. Spielman; plate provided by Faith Ogawa; shells provided by Alice and Ichiro Yamaguchi of Yamaguchi Farms, Kamuela, Big Island.

Minaka's Mac Nut Brownie

Serves 4

I really enjoy a good, crunchy-crusted, gooey brownie. So when my friend Minaka brought these brownies to a Christmas party, I asked her for the recipe. In my restaurants I top the brownies with two scoops of vanilla ice cream and a thin stream of chocolate syrup. It's a rich treat.

Brownies are great. They are a dessert that isn't really a cookie, and isn't really a cake. And it's not a fruit bar. The real secret to getting a crunchy outer crust with a gooey center is to slightly underbake the brownies.

1/2 cup dark or
  semi-sweet chocolate
1/2 cup butter, softened
3 eggs

1-1/4 cups granulated sugar
1 cup flour, sifted all-purpose
1 teaspoon vanilla extract
1/4 cup macadamia nuts, diced

Melt chocolate and butter in double boiler. Whip eggs with sugar for 5 to 10 minutes, until thick and a pale yellow color. Gradually stream chocolate into the egg mixture, and continue to whip. Fold flour into batter, and pour into greased, 8-by-8-inch pan. Sprinkle macadamia nuts on top, and bake at 325° for about an hour or until an inserted toothpick comes out almost clean. Cool. Top with vanilla ice cream before serving.

Garnish:

macadamia nuts
vanilla ice cream

Macadamia nuts provided by Alice and Ichiro Yamaguchi of Yamaguchi Farms, Kamuela, Big Island; ceramic tiles by artist Kyle Ino, Kaneʻohe, Oʻahu; plate donated by Liz Hersage of Prestige Designs Hawaii, Kamuela, Big Island; strawberries donated by Michael Prine of Strawberry Hawaii, Inc., Kamuela, Big Island.

Bermuda Triangle

1 ounce vodka
1 ounce pineapple juice
1 ounce orange juice
1 ounce grenadine
1 ounce sweet & sour juice
1 ounce Midori liquer
ice

Garnish:
1/4 of a pineapple slice
1 maraschino cherry

Fill hurricane glass with ice, then begin to build drink. Start with vodka, then add pineapple juice, orange juice, grenadine, and top with sweet & sour. Float with Midori, or top with a pineapple slice (quartered) and a maraschino cherry.

You Are the Bestest

1 ounce Kahlua
1 ounce Bailey's Irish Cream
1 ounce coconut syrup
1 ounce ripe banana
1 ounce half & half cream
ice

Garnish:
1 slice of banana
1/4 slice of pineapple

Fill blender with ice to 1/3-full. Add ingredients, and blend until creamy. Pour mixture into Reidel glass, and garnish with a slice of banana, and 1/4 slice of a pineapple.

Sam's North Shore Smoothie

1 ounce vodka
1 ounce orange juice
1 ounce cranberry juice
2 ounces strawberry purée
1 ounce Grenadine syrup
ice

Garnish:
3 tablespoons whipped cream
1 maraschino cherry

Fill blender with ice to 1/3-full. Add ingredients, and blend. Pour mixture into a Viva Grande glass, and top with whipped cream. Garnish with a maraschino cherry.

Scorpion in a Glass

1 ounce light rum
1 ounce brandy
2 ounces orange juice
1 ounce Orgeat syrup
ice

Garnish:
1/4 slice of orange

Fill blender with ice to a little less than 1/4-full. Add ingredients, and blend. Pour mixture into a champagne flute, and garnish with 1/4 slice of orange.

Haupia with a Kick, "Oh Yeah"

1 ounce light rum
2 ounces Coco Lopez coconut syrup
1 ounce half & half cream
ice

Garnish:
1 orchid

Fill blender with ice to 1/3-full. Blend all ingredients, then pour into Viva Grande glass, and garnish with an orchid.

Lava Flow–Get It While It's Hot!!!

2 ounces strawberry purée
1 ounce light rum
1 ounce pineapple juice
1 ounce sweet & sour juice
1 ounce coconut syrup
1 ounce half & half cream
ice

Garnish:
1/4 slice of pineapple
1 orchid

Pour strawberry purée into a 14-ounce hurricane glass. Fill blender with ice to 1/3-full, and add all other ingredients. Purée until slushy. Tilt hurricane glass to the side, and gently pour blender purée down the inside of the glass, careful not to disturb the strawberry purée.

Guava Colada from the Valley

1 ounce light rum
1 ounce pineapple juice
2 ounces guava juice (concentrate)
1 ounce Coco Lopez coconut syrup
1 ounce half & half cream
ice

Garnish:
1/4 of a pineapple slice
1 orchid

Fill blender with ice to 1/3-full. Add ingredients, and blend until slushy. Pour into hurricane glass, and garnish with a quarter of a pineapple slice and an orchid.

Kona Mac Freeze

1 ounce Kahlua
1 ounce Kahana Mac Nut Liqueur
1 ounce half & half cream
ice

Garnish:
3 tablespoons whipped cream
1 teaspoon ground macadamia nuts

Fill blender with ice to 1/3-full. Add ingredients, and blend until creamy. Pour into a Viva Grande glass to 1/4-inch from the top. Add whipped cream, and sprinkle with ground macadamia nuts.

Over the Rainbow

1 ounce Malibu rum
2 ounces pineapple juice
2 ounces cranberry juice
1 ounce Midori liqueur
ice

Garnish:
1/4 slice of pineapple
1 orchid

Fill hurricane glass with ice. Add ingredients. Float with 1 ounce of Midori liqueur, and garnish with 1/4 slice of pineapple and an orchid.

Loco Loco Mocha Mocha

1 ounce Coco Rum
1 ounce Kahlua
1 ounce half & half
3 ounces pineapple juice
1 ounce Kahuluacino
ice

Garnish:
3 tablespoons whipped cream
cocoa powder (for dusting)
1 maraschino cherry

Squirt chocolate syrup around the inside of a 14-ounce hurricane glass. Fill blender with ice to 1/3-full. Add ingredients, and blend until creamy. Pour into hurricane glass, leaving 1/4-inch at the top. Cap with whipped cream, and a dash of cocoa dust. Place cherry on whipped cream.

Tropical Crab Itch

1 ounce orange Curacao
2 ounces orange juice
1 ounce Orgeat syrup
1 ounce dark rum
ice

Garnish:
1/4 slice of pineapple
1 orchid
1 backscratcher (optional)

Fill blender with ice to 1/3-full. Add orange Curacao, orange juice, and Orgeat syrup. Blend until slushy, and pour into hurricane glass. Float with dark rum, and garnish with 1/4 slice of pineapple, an orchid, and a back scratcher!

Gallo Wine List

Recipe	Recommended Choice
1 Appetizers	
Breakfast, Lunch and Crab's Crab Cakes with Curry Aioli	Gossamer Bay White Zinfandel
Steamed Ama Ebi with Dipping Sauce	Gallo of Sonoma Chardonnay
'Ahi Tartare with Ginger	Tott's Brut
Lomi Lomi Spooned 'O'io (Bonefish)	Turning Leaf Chardonnay
Seafood-Stuffed 'Opelu with Tomato Lomi	Gossamer Bay Merlot
"Catch of the Day" Crispy Seafood Basket	Turning Leaf Sonoma Reserve Chardonnay
Breaded Oysters with Wasabi Cocktail Sauce	Indigo Hills Sauvignon Blanc
Ogo, Shrimp, and Scallop Tempura	Ecco Domani Merlot
Chinese Scallops with Chili-Ginger Oil and Black Beans	Gossamer Bay Chardonnay
Deep-Fried Crab Meat Balls with Sweet & Sour Pineapple Sauce	Gossamer Bay Sauvignon Blanc
Oyster Cakes with Hijimi Rémoulade	Turning Leaf Sonoma Reserve Chardonnay
Island-Style Stir-Fried Shrimp	Gossamer Bay Zinfandel
Lobster Boil with Hawaiian Salt, Chili Peppers & Other Stuffs	Gallo of Sonoma Chardonnay
Fresh Oysters w/Jicama and Fresh Chili Lime Shoyu	Ecco Domani Pinot Grigio
Oysters on the Half-Shell with Ginger Daikon Sauce	Ecco Domani Pinot Grigio
Steamed Clams and Shrimp with Spicy Black Beans	Turning Leaf Sonoma Reserve Pinot Noir
'Ahi Cakes with Wasabi Aioli	Turning Leaf Sonoma Reserve Pinot Noir
Furikake-Crusted Sashimi	Gallo of Sonoma Pinot Noir
2 Soups & Salads	
Dungeness Crab Soup	Gossamer Bay Sauvignon Blanc
'Ahi Salad with Creamy Peanut Dressing	Gossamer Bay White Zinfandel
Baby Romaine Lettuce with Honey Ginger Bay Scallops & Fresh Bay Shrimp	Ecco Domani Pinot Grigio
Spicy Soy Shrimp Salad	Turning Leaf Pinot Noir
Seafood Cream of Broccoli Soup	Gossamer Bay Sauvignon Blanc
Poached Scallops with a Tarragon Vinaigrette	Turning Leaf Sonoma Reserve Chardonnay
Cold Shrimp and Long Rice Salad	Turning Leaf Merlot
Wok-Fried Red Lettuce and Red Oak with Ginger Slivers, Garlic & Fried Shrimp	Gossamer Bay Merlot
Maui Fisherman's Soup	Indigo Hills Sauvignon Blanc
Macadamia Nut-Crusted Ono Caesar Salad	Gallo of Sonoma Chardonnay
Ginger Clam Miso Soup	Indigo Hills Brut

Recipe	Recommended Choice
Hot and Sour Opah Soup	Turning Leaf White Zinfandel
Green Papaya Abalone Soup	Ecco Domani Pinot Grigio
Sam's Shrimp and Papaya Salad	Anapamu Chardonnay
3 Pasta & Poke	
Kona Fisherman's Wife's Pasta	Ecco Domani Merlot
Chinese Pasta with Sesame-Crusted Opah	Gossamer Bay Merlot
Color Coa Poke with Red Ogo	Gallo of Sonoma Chardonnay
Tofu Poke with Red Ogo	Gossamer Bay Merlot
Marinated Poke in Coconut Milk	Indigo Hills Sauvignon Blanc
Spicy Poke	Gossamer Bay White Zinfandel
Shrimp Scampi with Green Linguini	Marcelina Chardonnay
Spaghetti with Seafood Tomato Sauce	Ecco Domani Merlot
Tropical Island Poke	Indigo Hills Brut
Smoked A'u Poke	Gallo Sonoma Chardonnay
Tomato Poke with Green Ogo and Dry 'Opae	Turning Leaf Merlot
"Ogo," You Go, I Go Oysters (Yummy)	Ecco Domani Pinot Grigio
Lobster Poke	Gossamer Bay Chardonnay
Poke Crabs Medley	Turning Leaf Chardonnay
Kona Cuisine Ulua Poke with Oriental Citrus Vinaigrette	Gossamer Bay Sauvignon Blanc
Lu'au Shrimp Pasta	Turning Leaf Chardonnay
4 Fish	
Macadamia Nut Mahimahi with Chili-Papaya-Pineapple Chutney	Turning Leaf Sonoma Reserve Chardonnay
Steamed Onaga with Pickled Ginger and Scallions	Ecco Domani Pinot Grigio
Blackened Ono	Gallo of Sonoma Cabernet
Seared Albacore Tuna with Coconut-Ginger Sauce	Gallo of Sonoma Pinot Noir
Weke 'Ula with Shoyu Ginger Sauce & Roasted Sesame Butter	Turning Leaf Chardonnay
Ginger Pesto Rice with Macadamia Nut Mahimahi	Gallo of Sonoma Pinot Noir
Miso Yaki Salmon	Gallo of Sonoma Pinot Noir
Onaga with Tropical Herb Salsa	Gallo of Sonoma Chardonnay
Fresh 'Ahi Clubhouse Sandwich	Gossamer Bay Merlot
Onaga with Tropical Sweet and Sour Sauce	Gossamer Bay Chardonnay
Sautééd Mahimahi with Warm Corn Sauce	Anapamu Chardonnay
Kuku's Pan-Fried Kalikali	Turning Leaf Pinot Noir
Ginger Pesto-Crusted 'Opakapaka with Coconut Cream Sauce	Indigo Hills Savignon Blanc
Crunchy Hale'iwa Mahimahi	Gallo of Sonoma Merlot

Recipe	Recommended Choice
Deep-Fried Hapuʻupuʻu (Sea Bass) with Tropical Fruit Salsa	Anapamu Chardonnay
Mahimahi Black Beans with Stir-Fried Vegetables	Turning Leaf Merlot

5 Shellfish

Recipe	Recommended Choice
Christopher's Crab Cakes with Herb Sauce	Gossamer Bay Chardonnay
Sam's "Local Boy" Cioppino	Gallo of Sonoma Chardonnay
Crab Omelette	Gossamer Bay White Zinfandel
Wok-Seared Ama Ebi with Lemon Grass	Indigo Hills Sauvignon Blanc
Seafood Creole	Ecco Domani Merlot
Oven-Roasted Dungeness Crab with Garlic Butter	Gallo of Sonoma Merlot
Lobster Club with Tango Lettuce	Turning Leaf Zinfandel
Panko Oysters with Spicy, Vine-Ripened Tomato Relish	Indigo Hills Sauvignon Blanc
Steamed Clams in Asian Broth	Ecco Domani Pinot Grigio
Seared Ginger Scallops with Tomato-Chanterelles Lomi	Turning Leaf Pinot Noir
Steamed Clams with Ginger Pesto Butter	Ecco Domani Pinot Grigio
Coconut Mac-Nut Shrimp with Guava Sweet & Sour Sauce	Gossamer Bay White Zinfandel
Steamed Maryland Blue Crabs	Turning Leaf Sonoma Reserve Chardonnay
Steamed "Ono-licious" Shrimp	Gallo of Sonoma Chardonnay
Scallops with Chinese Cabbage and Ramen	Marcelina Chardonnay

6 Barbecue

Recipe	Recommended Choice
Barbecued Aʻu (Swordfish) Kabobs	Gallo of Sonoma Pinot Noir
Broiled Lobster with Basil-Garlic Butter Sauce and Grilled Corn Relish	Anapamu Chardonnay
Creole Grilled Onaga	Gallo of Sonoma Chardonnay
Foil-Wrapped ʻOpelu	Turning Leaf Sonoma Reserve Chardonnay
Grilled Marinated Mahimahi with Poha, Mango, and Papaya Relish	Anapamu Chardonnay
Calamari with a Hibachi Twist	Gallo of Sonoma Merlot
Cilantro Salmon Steaks	Gallo of Sonoma Pinot Noir
ʻAhi with Lime-Shoyu Marinade	Ecco Domani Pinot Grigio
Broiled ʻOpakapaka	Indigo Hills Sauvignon Blanc
Grilled Mixed Seafood Salad	Turning Leaf Chardonnay
Fried ʻOpelu with Tomato-Ogo Relish	Ecco Domani Merlot or Ecco Domani Pinot Grigio
Grilled Basil-Ginger Aʻu Steaks	Gallo of Sonoma Cabernet
Mahimahi with Cilantro Chutney	Gallo of Sonoma Zinfandel

Recipe	Recommended Choice
Marinated Shrimp, Scallops, and Mango Kabobs	Gossamer Bay Chardonnay
Ono with Grilled Garden Vegetables	Ecco Domani Merlot
Poke Kabobs	Ecco Domani Merlot
Spicy Grilled Opah	Gossamer Bay White Zinfandel
Stuffed Calamari with Apple Banana & Cooked on the Hibachi	Gossamer Bay Zinfandel
Tequila-Grilled Shrimp	Turning Leaf Sonoma Reserve Chardonnay
Pulehu Island Mix Grill	Gallo of Sonoma Chardonnay

7 Sides & Stir-Fry

Recipe	Recommended Choice
Black Goma Asparagus with Bay Scallops	Gossamer Bay Sauvignon Blanc
Choy Sum with "Ono-licious" Sauce	Gossamer Bay Merlot
Honokaʻa-Style Bread Stuffing	Gossamer Bay Chardonnay
Baked Coconut Taro	Gossamer Bay Chardonnay
Kahuku Corn Smashed Potatoes	Turning Leaf Chardonnay
Kona Flaming Wok Clams in Shells	Gossamer Bay White Zinfandel
Hibachi Mixed Vegetables	Ecco Domani Pinot Grigio
Carrots and Cranberries	Gossamer Bay Merlot
Shiitake Mushroom Rice with Shredded Ono Stir-Fry and Fresh Spinach	Gallo of Sonoma Pinot Noir
Paniolo Potato Hash	Turning Leaf Sonoma Reserve Cabernet Sauvignon
Sam Choy's Lop Cheong Fried Rice	Turning Leaf Zinfandel
Steve's Kona Ogo Coleslaw	Gossamer Bay Sauvignon Blanc
Stir-Fried Chili-Garlic Shrimp	Gossamer Bay Chardonnay
Waipiʻo Hoʻiʻo Kim Chee	Gossamer Bay Merlot
Wok Lobster with Fresh Kona Oyster Mushrooms	Gallo of Sonoma Chardonnay
Stir-Fried Dungeness Crab and Black Beans	Turning Leaf Zinfandel

8 Desserts & Drinks

Recipe	Recommended Choice
Apple Cobbler	Cask & Cream
Chocolate, Chocolate-Chip Cheesecake	Ballatore
Coconut Bread Pudding	Ballatore
Crème Brûlée	Ballatore
Macadamia Nut Cream Pie	Ballatore
Sam Choy's Pineapple Cheesecake with Macadamia Nut Crust	Ballatore
Haupia Profiteroles	Ballatore
Lemon Tart	Ballatore
Macadamia Nut Banana Cake	Ballatore
Key Lime Pie	Ballatore
Minaka's Mac Nut Brownie	Ballatore

Artists' Credits

1 Appetizers

Steamed Ama Ebi with Dipping Sauce 4

Antique fishing net from Danny Akaka, Hawaiian Historian at the Mauna Lani Hotel, Kohala Coast, Big Island; Oriental bamboo steamer provided by Nancy James, Host Marriot Corp., Polynesian Cultural Center, La'ie, O'ahu; sauce bowl by Georgio Sartoris.

Seafood-Stuffed Opelu with Tomato Lomi 9

Fabric background by Jan of Hina Lei Creations, Kamuela, Big Island; carvings by Dean Ka'ahanui of Ka'ahanui Kreations, Kamuela, Big Island; wooden platter provided by Georgia Sartoris of Georgia Sartoris Fine Art, Pa'auilo, Big Island.

Ogo, Shrimp, and Scallop Tempura 12

Ceramic appetizer platter by artist Kyle Ino of Kaneohe, O'ahu; dipping saucer by Betsi Kohler of Betsi's Bowls of Volcano, Big Island; foliage donated by Eric S. Tanouye of Green Point Nursery, Hilo, Big Island; ogo provided by Steven A. Katase of Royal Hawaiian Sea Farms, Kailua-Kona, Big Island.

Oyster Cakes with Hijimi Rémoulade 16

Fabric design by Junko Week; plate provided by Liberty House; dipping dish by Betsi Kohler of Betsi's Bowls in Volcano on the Big Island; and flowers by Eric S. Tanouye of Green Point Nursery in Hilo, Big Island, and Kelvin T. Sewake, Hilo, Big Island.

Fresh Oysters with Jicama and Fresh Lime Chili Soy Sauce 20

Shooter glasses by glassetcher, Gary Wagner; nautical brass porthole provided by Mary &

Captain Mike Remer of Mariner's Canteen; painted wooden fish provided by Nancy James of Host Marriot's Shop Polynesia at the Polynesian Cultural Center.

2 Soups & Salads

'Ahi Salad with Creamy Peanut Dressing 30

Glass platter lent by Liz Hersage of Prestige Designs Hawai'i, Kamuela, Big Island; oyster mushrooms donated by Kona Mushrooms Inc., Kailua-Kona, Big Island; fish chopstick holders lent by Jeane Nakahara of Antique Sakae, Hilo, Big Island; chopsticks by John S. Pierl, lent by Volcano Art Gallery, Hawai'i National Park, Big Island; small sauce bowl made by artist Georgia Sartoris of Georgia Sartoris Fine Art, Pa'auilo, Big Island.

Seafood Cream of Broccoli Soup 35

Soup bowl provided by Liberty House, Honolulu, O'ahu; green fabric napkin lent by Brenda Schott of Under the Koa Tree, Waikoloa Resort, Big Island; koa bread board lent by Makana O Hawaii Gift Shop and made by Maika'i Wood Hawaii, Mauna Lani Bay Hotel and Bungalows, Big Island; flowers donated by Roen Hufford and Marie McDonald, Kamuela, Big Island; bread rolls donated Renee Dyer, Kailua-Kona, Big Island.

Poached Scallops with a Tarragon Vinaigrette 36

Etched green platter made by Jennifer Pontz of Tropical Art Glass, Holualoa, Big Island; flowers donated by Amy and Mike Rosato, Island Orchids, Kailua-Kona, Big Island.

Maui Fisherman's Soup 41

Bowl by Ronald Hanatani of RYH Pottery, Volcano, Big Island; starfish lent by Nancy

James of Host/Marriot, La'ie, O'ahu; shells provided by Pi'i Laeha, Laupahoehoe, Big Island; fabric donated by Mamo Howell, Inc., Honolulu, O'ahu.

Macadamia Nut-Crusted Ono Caesar Salad 42

Watercolor painting done by artist Candice Lee, Kamuela, Big Island; fabric by Hina Lei Creations, Kamuela, Big Island.

Green Papaya Abalone Soup 46

Green papaya turtle carving made by Raymond M. Yamasaki, of Ray's Oriental Designs, Kamuela, Big Island; anthuriums donated by Eric S. Tanouye of Green Point Nursery, Hilo, Big Island; antique bowl lent by Jean Nakahara of Antique Sakae, Hilo, Big Island; fabric by Hina Lei Creations, Kamuela, Big Island.

Sam's Shrimp and Papaya Salad 49

Martini etched glass and sauce containter made by Jennifer Pontz of Tropical Art Glass, Holualoa, Big Island; quilt by Bonnie Miki of Kona Kapa, Inc., Kailua-Kona, Big Island; lei made by Marie McDonald and Roen Hufford, Kamuela, Big Island.

3 Pasta & Poke

Chinese Pasta with Sesame-Crusted Opah 54

Ceramic plate by Ronald Y. Hanatani of RYH Pottery, Volcano, Big Island; ceramic vase and tiles by Kyle Ino of Kyle Ino Designs, Kaneohe, O'ahu; flowers donated by Marie McDonald and Roen Hufford, Kamuela, Big Island.

Spicy Poke 59

Mahalo to Levina Wong, Liberty House Special Events Coordinator and Carlos Hernandez, Culinary Advisor, Liberty House—Ala Moana for allowing us to use the dishes and glass fish in this photo.

Tropical Island Poke 62

Hand-made paper by Lisa Adams of Spiral Triangle Studios, Volcano, Big Island; bowl made by artist Renee Fukumoto-Ben, Kailua-Kona, Big Island; lei provided by Tom Pico of Gallerie of Great Things, Volcano, Big Island.

Lu'au Shrimp Pasta 68

Coconut placemat from Peggy Chesnut of Chesnut and Company, Holualoa, Big Island; fabric by Hina Lei Creations, Kamuela, Big Island; ceramic plate by R. Jeff Lee of Lee Ceramics, Waialua, O'ahu; flowers donated by Eric S. Tanouye of Green Point Nursery, Hilo, Big Island.

4 Fish

Seared Albacore Tuna with Coconut-Ginger Sauce 77

Plate provided by Liberty House—Ala Moana, Honolulu, O'ahu; flowers donated by Amy and Mike Rosato of Island Orchid, Kailua-Kona, Big Island; fabric by Jan of Hina Lei Creations, Kamuela, Big Island; greenery donated by Eric S. Tanouye of Green Point Nursery, Hilo, Big Island.

Miso Yaki Salmon 80

Plate provided by Sam Choy; salt and pepper shakers provided by Rick Clark, Kailua-Kona, Big Island; orchids donated by James McCully Orchids Culture, Hakalau, Big Island.

Onaga with Tropical Sweet and Sour Sauce 85

Platter by artist Tom Pico lent by The Gallery of Great Things, Kamuela, Big Island; lauhala mats provided by Auntie Elizabeth Lee of Malu's Enterprise, Kailua-Kona, Big Island.

Ginger Pesto-Crusted 'Opakapaka with Coconut Cream Sauce 88

Plate by Ronald Y. Hanatani of RYH Pottery, Volcano, Big Island; feather lei lent by Danny Akaka, Hawaiian Historian at the Mauna Lani Hotel, Kohala Coast, Big Island; wooden serving tray lent by Liberty House-Ala Moana, Honolulu, O'ahu; ti leaf lei made by Amy and Mike Rosato, Island Orchid, Kailua-Kona, Big Island; vine-ripened tomatoes by Nakano Farms, Waimea, Big Island.

Mahimahi Black Beans with Stir-Fried Vegetables 93

Plate provided by Liberty House —Ala Moana, Honolulu, O'ahu; flowers donated by Eric S. Tanouye of Green Point Nursery, Hilo, Big Island.

5 Shellfish

Sam's "Local Boy" Cioppino 99

Bowl provided by Faith Ogawa of Faith and Friends, Kamuela, Big Island; salt and pepper shaker lent by Rick Clark of Hawaiiana Vintage Collector, Kailua-Kona, Big Island; fabric by Hina Lei Creations, Kamuela, Big Island; napkin ring by Pi'i Laehe, Laupahoehoe, Big Island; napkin lent by Brenda Schott of Under the Koa Tree, Waikoloa Resort, Big Island.

Seafood Creole 103

Ceramic bowl made by artist Ed Enomoto, Kula, Maui; flowers donated by Alice Ichiro and Deedee Yamaguchi, Kamuela, Big Island.

Steamed Clams in Asian Broth 106

Bowl made by R. Jeff Lee of Lee Ceramics, Waialua, O'ahu, flowers donated by Momi Greene of Greene Acres, Kailua-Kona, Big Island.

Coconut Mac-Nut Shrimp with Guava Sweet & Sour Sauce 111

Papier mâché background by Terry Taube, Kailua-Kona, Big Island; square ceramic platter lent by Hilton Waikaloa Village, Waikaloa, Big Island; carrot flower carving donated by Raymond M. Yamasaki of Ray's Oriental Designs, Kamuela, Big Island; sauce container by Georgia Sartoris of Georgia Sartoris Fine Art, Pa'auilo, Big Island; flowers donated by James McCully Orchid Culture, Hakalau, Big Island.

Scallops with Chinese Cabbage and Ramen 114

Ceramic platter lent by Hilton Waikaloa Village, Waikaloa, Big Island; pipipi shell lei lent by Patrick Choy, Honolulu, O'ahu.

6 Barbecue

Broiled Lobster with Basil-Garlic Butter and Grilled Corn Relish 120

Fluted koa platter piece by Gerald Ben, artwork provided by Chesnut & Company, Holualoa, Big Island; antique tapa lent by Mindy Raymond; etched gourd made by Momi Greene of Greene Acres, Kailua-Kona, Big Island.

Grilled Marinated Mahimahi with Poha, Mango, and Papaya Relish 125

Plate provided by Liberty House; scarf provided by Liberty House-Kona; poha berries donated by Alice and Ichiro Yamaguchi, Kamuela, Big Island.

Grilled Mixed Seafood Salad 130

"Hibiscus" quilt by Bonnie Miki of Kona Kapa, Inc., Kailua-Kona, Big Island; etched glass platter by Gary Wagner, Kamuela Island; napkin ring made by Pi'i Laeha; napkin lent by Under the Koa House Gallery, Waikoloa Resort.

Ono with Grilled Garden Vegetables 137

Lava sculpture by Terry Taube, Kailua-Kona, Big Island; plate donated by Faith Ogawa, Kamuela, Big Island; fabric by Jan of Hina Lei Creations, Kamuela, Big Island; flowers provided by Roen Hufford, Kamuela, Big Island.

Pulehu Island Mix Grill 142

Chef Sam Choy's hibachi; chili pepper water bottle provided by Jennifer Pontz of Tropical Art Glass, Holualoa, Big Island.

7 Sides & Stir-Fry

Carrots and Cranberries (photographed with Baked Taro) 155

Bronze poi pounder done by Stephen Kofsky of Kofsky Fine Arts, Kailua-Kona, Big Island; bowls lent by Liberty House—Ala Moana; lei made by Norman "Buzzy" Histo of Kalikokalehua Hula Studio, Kamuela, Big Island; koa wood sashimi platform lent by Liberty House—Kailua-Kona, Big Island.

Shiitake Mushroom Rice with Shredded Ono Stir-Fry and Fresh Spinach 156

Wok provided by Liberty House; flowers donated by Norman "Buzzy" Histo of Kalikokalehua Hula Studio, Kamuela, Big Island.

Steve's Kona Ogo Coleslaw 161

Etched glass bowl made by Gary Wagner of Plaza Pacific Design, Kamuela, Big Island; etched glass balls made by Jennifer Pontz of Tropical Art Glass, Holualoa, Big Island.

Stir-Fried Dungeness Crab and Black Beans 164

Plate etched by Jennifer Pontz of Tropical Art Glass, Holualoa, Big Island; fabric designed by Hina Lei Creations, Kamuela, Big Island; flower vase by Kyle Ino of Kyle Ino Designs, Kaneohe, O'ahu; flowers donated by Marie McDonald.

8 Desserts & Drinks

Crème Brûlée 172

Painted wooden fish provided by Nancy James, Host Marriot Corp., Polynesian Cultural Center, La'ie, O'ahu; bowl provided by Liberty House—Ala Moana, Honolulu, O'ahu; plate provided by Kevin P. Nut, West Hawaii Foodworks, Kamuela, Big Island; fabric by Jan of Hina Lei Creations, Kamuela, Big Island.

Haupia Profiteroles 177

Plate provided by Liberty House—Ala Moana, Honolulu, O'ahu; flowers donated by Harvey and Denise Truck, Hilo, Big Island; strawberries by Michael Prine of Strawberry Hawaii, Inc., Kamuela, Big Island.

Key Lime Pie 180

Kou paddle by artist J.K. Spielman; plate provided by Faith Ogawa; shells provided by Alice and Ichiro Yamaguchi of Yamaguchi Farms, Kamuela, Big Island.

Minaka's Mac Nut Brownie 183

Macadamia nuts provided by Alice and Ichiro Yamaguchi of Yamaguchi Farms, Kamuela, Big Island; ceramic tiles by artist Kyle Ino, Kaneohe, O'ahu; plate lent by Liz Hersage of Prestige Designs Hawaii, Kamuela, Big Island; strawberries donated by Michael Prine of Strawberry Hawaii, Inc., Kamuela, Big Island.

Glossary

Abalone—a marine mollusk with an "ear-shaped" shell that is often used in Oriental-style salads and stir-fries.

'Ahi—Hawaiian name for tuna: "yellowfin," "bigeye," or "Albacore."

'Alaea salt—Hawaiian rock salt.

Ama ebi—very large shrimp, locally harvested off the coast of Kaua'i.

A'u—Hawaiian name for billfish; marlin or swordfish.

Balsalmic vinegar—top-quality balsamic vinegar is made by harvesting and fermenting very ripe sweet white grapes. The fermentation process takes 4-5 years, producing a very dark brown liquid with a somewhat syrupy consistency.

Basmati rice—an aged short-grain rice used in Indian cooking and Middle Eastern dishes.

Bay scallops—these small scallops are often used in Chinese stir-fry because of their size and delicate flavor.

Black beans—small fermented black beans preserved in salt, and used to flavor Chinese sauces.

Black goma—black sesame seeds.

Calamari—Italian name for squid. Commonly called by its Japanese name "tako" here in Hawai'i.

Chili-Tamarind Paste—tamarind, the fruit of a Southeast Asian legume, is made into a paste, and mixed with hot chili paste. Found in the Oriental sections of most local supermarkets.

Cilantro—Chinese parsley.

Coconut Milk—the liquid extracted by squeezing the grated meat of a coconut.

Daikon—a white-fleshed Asian root that can grow to a length of 14 inches and weigh a hefty 4 to 5 pounds. Used in Japan for soups, pickles, or eaten raw.

Dashi—a clear, light Japanese broth. Sold as instant stock in granules or tea-bags. Substitute with chicken stock.

Dungeness crab—large, meaty crab harvested off the West Coast, British Columbia, and Alaska. Sold frozen, previously frozen, or fresh.

Furikake—Japanese condiment of dried seaweed flakes and sesame seeds, available in the Asian section of local supermarkets.

Ginger—spicy, pungent rhizome.

Hawaiian chili pepper—small, potently hot chili pepper grown and used widely in Hawai'i.

Hawaiian chili pepper water—water infused with the oils from fiery hot Hawaiian chili peppers and vinegar.

Hawaiian salt—white or pink coarse sea salt traditionally harvested on Kaua'i.

Hibachi—small, portable, inexpensive Japanese outdoor grill used widely in back-yards, on patios, and at beaches in Hawai'i.

Hijimi—spicy, Japanese pepper sprinkle.

Ho'i'o—Hawaiian name for edible fern shoots.

'Inamona—traditional Hawaiian condiment made of roasted, ground, and salted kukui nut meat; used to flavor poke.

Jicama—crunchy root vegetable that is eaten raw or cooked, Chinese yam.

Kalikali—Hawaiian name for "red-tail snapper" or a small 'opakapaka.

Kim chee—a hot, pungent pickled cabbage mixture basic to Korean cooking.

Lemon Grass—a citrus-scented grass that adds a distinctive lemon flavor and aroma to the cooking of Indonesia, Malaysia, Indochina, and Thailand. Its long, woody stalk grows from a base that resembles the white part of a green onion.

Limu—Hawaiian word for "seaweed."

Lop Cheong—Chinese pork sausage.

Kamaboko—Japanese red or white fish cakes made of puréed white fish mixed with potato starch and salt, then steamed.

Lu'au—young taro leaves; cook thoroughly 50-60 minutes before eating; used in laulau; has come to mean a "feast" where laulau is traditionally served.

Macadamia nuts—round, oily nut with a creamy, slightly crunchy texture; grows on trees mostly on the Big Island.

Mahimahi—Hawaiian name for "dolphinfish."

Mango—oval tropical fruit with golden-orange flesh and an enticing, aromatic flavor; skin color ranges from yellow-orange to burgundy to green; from a quarter-pound up in size; available in the produce section of markets; can substitute peaches or nectarines in recipes.

Maryland Blue crab—caught off the Atlantic coast. Sold in Hawai'i frozen, previously frozen, or as canned crabmeat.

Mirin—sweet rice wine. Substitute 1 table-spoon cream sherry or 1 teaspoon sugar for each tablespoon mirin.

Miso—soy bean paste made from fermented soybeans mixed with crushed grain. There are two types: white miso made from rice, and red miso, made from barley.

Moonfish—Opah

Mussels—imported to Hawai'i from New Zealand, are sold in local supermarkets frozen, previously frozen, or canned.

Nori—known as sushi paper, nori is dried seaweed that is sold in sheets or strips.

Ogo—Japanese name for Gracilaria seaweed.

Onaga—Japanese name for "red snapper." The Hawaiian name is 'ula'ula.

Ono—Hawaiian name for a large "mackerel," also known in Hawai'i as "Wahoo."

'Opae—general Hawaiian term for shrimp. Term used for packaged dry red shrimp.

Opah—French name for "moonfish."

'Opakapaka—Hawaiian name for "pink snapper."

'Opelu—Hawaiian name for a "mackerel scad."

'Opihi—limpet that is eaten raw; grows on rocks, often in high-wave areas; the fresh delicacy is prized at feasts.

Oyster sauce—a thick brown sauce with the subtle flavor of oysters. Used in many stir-fried dishes.

Panko—Japanese coarse bread crumbs used for crunchy deep-fried coatings.

Papaya—melon-like fruit with a smooth, yellow or orange flesh and a shiny green to yellow skin. Usually about one pound in weight.

Pipi Kaula—salted and spiced dried beef. Literal Hawaiian translation: rope beef.

Poha—yellow, cherry-size fruit with a spicy pulp and lantern-like parchment covering; rare in Hawai'i; known elsewhere as cape gooseberry, ground cherry, or husk tomato.

Poke—Hawaiian word for "slice"; refers to a traditional Hawaiian dish of sliced raw seafood, fresh seaweed, Hawaiian salt, and Hawaiian red chili peppers.

Portuguese sausage—a popular meaty product with mild, medium, or hot spicing; substitute Italian sausage.

Rice vinegar—Japan's relatively mild rice vinegar is the type most often found in local supermarkets. Chinese rice vinegar—white, red, or black—has a stronger flavor.

Sambal oelek—fiery-hot chili paste. A table condiment in Indonesia.

Sea scallops—large scallops harvested in the Atlantic from Labrador to New Jersey.

Sesame oil—this seasoning oil of China, Japan, and Korea is pressed from toasted sesame seeds into an aromatic, golden brown oil.

Shiitake mushrooms—from Japan and Korea, this meaty, dark mushroom is usually dried, then soaked to moisten before using. It is available fresh.

Somen noodles—these delicate Japanese noodles are usually produced from hard wheat flour mixed with oil. Most somen are white, but you'll sometimes see a yellow variety that contains egg yolks.

Shoyu—Dark, savory, and salty, shoyu (soy sauce) is one of the more versatile and frequently used Oriental seasonings. Made of soy beans, flour, yeast, salt, and sugar; saltiness varies from brand to brand.

Sugar snap peas—delightfully sweet pea, which is a cross between the English pea and the Chinese snow pea.

Sweet bread—sweet egg bread, also known as Hawaiian sweet bread or Easter bread.

Taro—nutritious, starchy tuber used for making poi, the traditional Hawaiian staple; more than 200 taro varieties are grown worldwide; steam, boil, or bake taro thoroughly 20-90 minutes, depending on size.

Thai Fish Sauce—a thin, salty, brownish gray sauce. Known as "nam pla" in Thailand, this particular type of fish sauce is much milder than the Japanese, Chinese, Burmese, or Vietnamese versions.

Tofu—fresh soybean curd; bland and therefore versatile.

Ulua—a crevally. Hawaiians gave names to the different stages of growth: papio, pau u'u, and ulua.

Wasabi—pungent root with an extremely strong, sharp flavor. Tastes something like horseradish. Available in powder form and paste.

Weke 'ula—Hawaiian name for "red surmullet."

Wok—versatile round-bottomed pan universal in Chinese cookery; used with and without a cover for stir-frying, steaming, boiling, braising, and deep-frying.

Won bok cabbage—Chinese cabbage.

Won ton—these "skins" are used in Oriental cooking for dishes like deep-fried won ton. They can be purchased in the Oriental section of most markets, and should be stored in a refrigerator in an airtight wrapping.

Sam Choy

Raised by an extended family of Hawaiian surfers, beach combers, and fishermen, Sam Choy was born to the water.

On a crescent of pristine blue called La'ie Bay, Sam spent many of his summer mornings, the early hours of "small-kid time," in a simple boat house with a palm-thatched roof. Here he wandered through the tropical shadows, surrounded by the smells and glowing colors of freshly caught fish, crab, and spiny lobster. This is where Sam learned the deep glory of the reefs, and the sweet sustenance of a craftsmanlike harvest.

The ancient husbandry of Hawai'i had imbued the men that worked the waters of La'ie Bay with a keen understanding of renewal: you fish for what the sea will give you, and if you wait for as long as it takes—knowing how the young fry will grow—there will always be plenty.

Every Saturday, Sam helped his dad, Sam Choy, Sr., prepare local delicacies like kalua pig, squid lu'au, lomi lomi salmon, and homemade haupia for the more than 800 tourists who came to the big lu'aus at La'ie's famous Hukilau. Of those days, Sam says, "The best part was pulling in the hukilau net. We did it to show the tourists how we caught fish, but then we got to take a lot of the catch home. After working hard all day, Dad cooked up the weke, papio, and other fish caught in the net, and we'd sit down and eat. Those were great times."

Sam grew up to become a world class chef, and one of his specialties, quite naturally, was seafood. He trained at the North Shore's Kuilima Resort (now the Turtle Bay Hilton), the Waldorf Astoria in New York City, and the Kona Hilton on the Big Island. After leaving his post as executive chef at the Kona Hilton, Sam opened Sam Choy's Diner at the Frame 10 Center. In 1996 he closed

the Diner and opened his family-style restaurant, Sam Choy's Kaloko Restaurant just outside of Kona.

By the end of 1997. Sam had three more restaurants—his fine-dining eatery, Sam Choy's Diamond Head Restaurant on Kapahulu Avenue in Honolulu; Sam Choy's Breakfast, Lunch and Crab, a micro-brewery and restaurant in Iwilei on Nimitz Highway next to Honolulu Harbor (it serves the city's freshest seafood); and Sam Choy's Tokyo at Sunset Beach Restaurant Row in Tokyo, Japan.

In 1998, Sam added restaurants on Maui and the mainland, opening Sam Choy's Kahului at the Ka'ahumanu Center on Maui, Sam Choy's Firecracker Restaurant in Kahului, and Sam Choy's Hawai'i at the Bali Hai at Shelter Island in San Diego.

Each restaurant has its own identity, with some very important elements that tie them all together: Sam's love for Island cuisine, his charming way of making people happy, and his ingenious methods for preparing Hawai'i's renowned seafood.

Sam still lives in Kailua-Kona on the Big Island with his wife Carol, his two sons, Sam Jr. and Christopher, and his Basenji Hoku and all of her five puppies (which the family couldn't bear to sell): Sally, Sassy, Jerry, Wednesday, and Bruddah.

Sam Choy's Souvenirs

All prices and availability are subject to change. All sales are final. Please contact any of Sam's Hawai'i restaurants for information, ordering, and current pricing.

PROFESSIONAL KITCHENWARE

Kona Flaming Wok $19.50
aluminum wok cover $5.99
stainless steel wok ladle $7.99
stainless steel wok turner $7.99
entire wok set $37.50

"LET'S EAT" WEAR*

cotton crew neck t-shirt $16.00
cotton scoop neck t-shirt $16.00
butcher-style apron $15.00
Diamond Head caps $15.00

"NEVER TRUST A SKINNY CHEF" WEAR

cotton crew neck t-shirt $16.00
butcher-style apron $16.00
Sam Choy's polo shirts $28.00

SPECIALTY FOOD ITEMS

Sam Choy's Volcano Roast Coffee (8 oz.) $7.99
Chef Sam's Creamy Oriental Dressing (12 oz.) $3.79

*Only available only at Sam Choy's Diamond Head Restaurant

Sam Choy's Diamond Head Restaurant
449 Kapahulu Avenue, Suite 201
Honolulu, HI 96815
Tel: (808) 732-8645
Fax: (808) 732-8683

Sam Choy's Kahului
275 Ka'ahumanu Avenue
Kahului, HI 96732
Tel: (808) 893-0366
Fax: (808) 893-0112

Sam Choy's Breakfast, Lunch & Crab
580 North Nimitz Hwy.
Honolulu, HI 96817
Tel: (808) 545-7979
Fax: (808) 531-3887

Sam Choy's Kaloko
73-5576 Kauhola Street
Kailua-Kona, HI 96740
Tel: (808) 326-1545
Fax: (808) 334-1230

SAM CHOY'S
DIAMOND HEAD · Lae 'ahi

"NEVER TRUST A SKINNY CHEF"

SAM CHOY
DIAMOND HEAD
Lae 'ahi

WITH SAM CHOY

THE CHOY OF COOKING

SAM CHOY'S
DIAMOND HEAD
Lae 'ahi

Sam Choy's
Breakfast,
Lunch & Crab
Honolulu, Hawaii

ROYAL KONA
WORLD CLASS COFFEE

SAM CHOY'S
KONA CUISINE

SAM CHOY'S
KONA CUISINE
Original
Oriental Dressing
NET WT 12 FL OZ (354 ML)

Biographies

U'i and Steven Goldsberry began collaborating on a series of writing projects three years ago, after their children graduated from Kahuku High School. U'i's work has appeared in a number of fitness magazines, and she recently completed a series of mini-travelogues for Mutual Publishing. Steven, an English Professor at the University of Hawai'i, is the award-winning author of *Maui the Demigod, Over Hawai'i*, and *Luzon*. His writing has appeared in the *New Yorker, The American Poetry Review, The Iowa Review, McCall's, Honolulu, Aloha*, and *GEO*.

Leo Gonzalez is the principal and creative director at Gonzalez Design Company. His firm designs promotional, corporate literature and identity for local, national, and international corporations, institutions and individuals. He has art directed and designed numerous award winning coffee table books including *The Choy of Cooking*. His accomplishments include prestigious recognitions and awards from the New York Art Directors Club, Print's Regional Design Annual, and the Honolulu Advertising Federation's Pele Awards. He worked for several New York City and Honolulu agencies and design firms and co-founded other companies before forming Gonzalez Design Company in 1993.

Faith Ogawa is a chef, food designer, promoter and coordinator of island food events, and enjoys sharing energy work (healing touch) with many. She has been a consultant to the nutritional service department of North Hawaii Community Hospital, a progressive, state-of-the-art facility that honors complementary healing techniques. Ogawa specializes in "healthful cuisine with the spirit of aloha." Her company Faith and Friends is involved in working with local vendors and artists in creating unique gift items from the islands.

She resides in Waimea, Big Island with her 13 year old son, Kahlil Dean. She holds a food service degree from Leeward Community College. Ogawa is on the advisory board for Kapiolani Community College Culinary Program. She is on the board of directors with the Chef DeCuisine, Kona Chapter. She was also the food and prop stylist for *With Sam Choy: Cooking from the Heart* and *The Choy of Cooking*.

Douglas Peebles has photographed a number of books on Hawai'i for Mutual Publishing—*From The Skies of Paradise* series, *Landmark Hawai'i, Hawai'i: A Floral Paradise, With Sam Choy: Cooking from the Heart, The Choy of Cooking*, and *The Choy of Seafood*, his third cookbook project. His newspaper and magazine credits include the *New York Times, Los Angeles Times, National Geographic, Condé-Nast Traveler*, and *Travel Holiday*. Peebles is originally from Jacksonville, Florida, and has lived in Hawai'i for 24 years. He, wife Margaret, sons Brad and Kevin, and two dogs live in Kailua, O'ahu.

The team: (standing l–r) **Chef Paul Muranaka, Kevin Nutt, Steven Goldsberry, Leo Gonzalez, Douglas Peebles, Raymond Wong,** (seated) **Renee Dyer, U'i Goldsberry, Faith Ogawa**

Index

❖ identifies entries with photos

Index (continued)